THE MAN WHO MET GOD IN A BAR

THE MAN WHO WHO MET GOD IN A BAR

THE GOSPEL ACCORDING TO MARVIN

a novel

ROBERT FARRAR CAPON

RICHELIEU COURT

ALBANY • NEW YORK

Richelieu Court Publications Inc.
8 Leesome Lane
P.O. Box 522-A
Altamont, New York 12009

Inquiries may be directed to:
The Publisher
Richelieu Court
P.O. Box 126
Kendall Park, New Jersey 08824

This is a work of fiction. Names, characters, places and incidents are either the product of the author's imagination or are used fictitiously.

Library of Congress Cataloging-in-Publication Data

Capon, Robert Farrar.
    The man who met God in a bar : the gospel according to
Marvin : a novel / Robert Farrar Capon.
        p.   cm.
    ISBN 0-911519-22-X : $15.95
    I. Title.
PS3553.A587M36   1990
813'.54—dc20   89-78168
                                                          CIP

Printed in the United States of America

For Leo—
who started it all

ἡ δ'ἀρχὴ λέγεται ἥμισυ εἶναι παντός

Overture

The scene is a cocktail lounge in the Cleveland airport at five o'clock on a Friday morning. A young man of about twenty-eight, dressed in a gray sweatshirt and white painter's pants, is sitting at the bar nursing a Coke, when Marvin G., a businessman who has just missed the red-eye flight from LA to New York, enters and sits down a few stools away.

MARVIN *(after much looking around and drumming of fingers)*: Hey! Is this place closed, or what? Bad enough I miss my plane without dying of thirst besides.

YOUNG MAN: Don't worry. It's open. The bartender just went to the john.

MARVIN: How long ago was that?

YOUNG MAN: Three, maybe four minutes. *(He drains the Coke can, sucking noisily through the straw.)* You want to play a game while you wait?

MARVIN: What kind of game?

YOUNG MAN: Spelling.

MARVIN *(thinks, then shrugs)*: Sure, why not? How does it go?

YOUNG MAN: Simple. You spell a word right and I buy you five drinks.

MARVIN: What's the catch? It's a foreign word?

YOUNG MAN: No, English. You even know it already.

MARVIN *(thinks again)*: How many chances do I get?

YOUNG MAN: All you want. The only thing is, every time you miss, I owe you one less drink. Over five mistakes, you start owing me.

MARVIN: Can I stop any time I want?

YOUNG MAN: Sure. You ready?

MARVIN: What's the word?

YOUNG MAN: You know Myers's Rum?

MARVIN: Of course.

YOUNG MAN: Spell "Myers's."

MARVIN: Sounds fair enough. (*He runs his eye over the bottles behind the bar.*)

YOUNG MAN: Don't bother looking. It's already turned sideways. Spell.

MARVIN: m-e-y-e-r-apostrophe-s.

YOUNG MAN: Wrong. I only owe you four.

MARVIN: What? Capital M, I suppose?

YOUNG MAN: Still wrong.

MARVIN: Did that count as a turn?

YOUNG MAN: Nah. I assumed you meant capital. Go again.

MARVIN: M-e-y-e-r-s-apostrophe?

YOUNG MAN: Wrong. Three.

MARVIN: You sure? M-e-i-e-r . . . ?

YOUNG MAN: Sure I'm sure. And that's wrong too.

MARVIN: M-y-e-r-s?

YOUNG MAN: Nope. Don't be in such a rush. You've only got one drink left.

MARVIN (*thinks*): M-y-e-r-apostrophe-s?

YOUNG MAN: Wrong again. We're zero, zero. You wanna quit? (*The Bartender returns.*)

MARVIN: No, I'm a sport. Besides, there's only one more thing it could be: M-y-e-r-s-apostrophe!

YOUNG MAN: 'Fraid not. You owe me one.

MARVIN: Come on! M-i-r-e-apostrophe-s?

YOUNG MAN: Listen. You better stop. You're getting wild. Two for me.

MARVIN: Okay. I give up. How's it spelled?

YOUNG MAN: M-y-e-r-s-apostrophe-s. Henry, show him the bottle.

MARVIN: (*inspects it and shakes his head*): Just think. All these years I've been looking at this . . . Oh, well. What'll you have?

YOUNG MAN: A Coke.

MARVIN: You sure you don't want something better? After all, you won.

YOUNG MAN: No. A Coke's fine.

MARVIN: Don't hold back on my account. I'm good for it.

YOUNG MAN: Well . . . okay then. I'll have a Ballantine's 30 year old.

MARVIN: (*to Bartender*): Make that two Ballantine's 30 year . . . (*he hesitates*) Er, wait a minute, Henry . . . what does that stuff go for?

BARTENDER: Ten dollars a shot.

MARVIN: Ten dollars! (*to Young Man*) You set me up!

YOUNG MAN: What do you mean, set you up? You twisted my arm to have something better than a Coke.

MARVIN: Not *that* much better.

YOUNG MAN: What happened to "Don't hold back on my account"?

MARVIN: That's got nothing to do with it. There are just some things people don't do when they're only kidding around.

YOUNG MAN: Who's only kidding? You mean if you'd won on the first shot you wouldn't have taken me for five drinks?

MARVIN: Well, sure . . . but I'd have ordered something reasonable . . . like, say, a Dewar's.

YOUNG MAN: Did we agree it had to be reasonable? Why not a Coke then instead of a Dewar's?

MARVIN: Cause I'd rather have a Dewar's.

YOUNG MAN: Well then, I'd rather have a Ballantine's 30. What's wrong with that?

MARVIN: It's not what a person would expect, that's what. (*To Bartender*) Listen, Henry. How many people come in here and order 30-year-old stuff?

BARTENDER: Only him.

MARVIN: What is this? You two got some kind of con going?

BARTENDER: Don't look at me, Mister. All I get is $4.50 an hour and tips. I just go along with his routine for kicks. As a matter of fact, that's all it's good for. Most guys get so mad they don't leave a tip.

MARVIN: Serves you right. (*Moodily*) Give him his drink; I'll have a Dewar's.

YOUNG MAN: Listen. Don't sweat it. You didn't like that game, I'll play you another: I'll buy us both a Dewar's if you can name all the gizmos on the Highlander's costume. I'll even spot you two gizmos: the oatmeal bag is a sporran and the sword is a claymore.

MARVIN: What do you think I am, crazy? You're not gonna sucker me twice.

YOUNG MAN: Okay then. How about a third game? You just say your name and I'll buy *you* a Ballantine's 30.

MARVIN: That's nuts!

YOUNG MAN: What's nuts? Henry! One Ballantine's 30 for the gentleman if he says his name.

MARVIN: This is crazy. I don't like it.

YOUNG MAN: Why? Is your name some kind of secret?

MARVIN: No. It's just that . . .

YOUNG MAN: What? I offer you a drink of the best stuff here and you won't even tell me your name? How come? It's not worth that kind of money? Would you tell it to me for a Dewar's?

MARVIN: That's got nothing to do with it.

YOUNG MAN: For a Coke, maybe?

MARVIN: This is silly.

YOUNG MAN: For nothing, then. What's your name?

MARVIN (*frowns*): Well . . . only if you tell me yours, too.

YOUNG MAN: I will, I will. Go ahead.

MARVIN (*thinks*): Is it still good for a drink?

YOUNG MAN: Sure.

MARVIN: Could I ask what kind?

YOUNG MAN: The same kind we agreed to before you got spooked: anything you want.

MARVIN: Even the 30-year-old stuff?

YOUNG MAN: Even that. C'mon. What's your name?

MARVIN: Well . . . it's Marvin. (*He frowns again.*) Do I have to tell you my last name?

YOUNG MAN: What's with this "have to" business?

MARVIN: I'm just being careful. Is Marvin enough?

YOUNG MAN: If you say so, Marvin. (*To Bartender*) One Ballantine's 30 for Marvin here, Henry, and one Coke for me.

MARVIN: Not so fast. You still didn't tell me your name. You promised.

YOUNG MAN: Only that I would. I didn't say when.

MARVIN: But *now* is when you should . . . before the drinks.

YOUNG MAN: Where do you get so many rules from, Marvin? You own a commandment factory or something? (*The drinks arrive.*) Take a sip at least. I hear it's terrific.

MARVIN: What do you mean, hear? I thought you drank this all the time.

YOUNG MAN: You don't listen to your own questions, Marvin. You asked Henry if I *ordered* it, not if I drank it. As a matter of fact, I've never even tasted the stuff. But never mind. Drink up.

MARVIN (*tastes it*): Holy cow! That's fabulous!

YOUNG MAN: You think maybe I could have a sip?

MARVIN: Well . . . I don't know.

YOUNG MAN: What's the matter? I'm being pushy?

MARVIN: No. It's just that you still haven't told me your name.

YOUNG MAN: But we never said no sips unless I told you my name.

MARVIN: Still, fair's fair.

YOUNG MAN: You're sitting there with a whole ten dollar shot because
I let you off a bet, and suddenly a sip is unfair?

MARVIN (*thinks*): Oh, I suppose you're right . . . It's just that I really
would like to know your name.

YOUNG MAN: Well! Why didn't you say that in the first place? My
name is God.

MARVIN: C'mon, cut the clowning.

YOUNG MAN: Did I say that to you when you told me "Marvin"?

MARVIN: No. But "God" . . . that's crazy.

YOUNG MAN: Why? "Marvin" is some kind of triumph of reasonable-
ness?

MARVIN: But you've got to be kidding.

YOUNG MAN: I'm not. Just call me God.

MARVIN: That's ridiculous. Who'd give a kid a name like God?

YOUNG MAN: Well, for one thing, any family whose last name was
already God.

MARVIN: You mean God isn't your first name? At least that makes a
little more sense.

YOUNG MAN: Your name is Marvin, and you can make distinctions
like that?

MARVIN: But still . . .

YOUNG MAN: Still what? Would it be better if I told you my name was
Dio?

MARVIN (*brightening*): Oh, I get it. Your family's Italian! You really had me going for a minute there, Pal.

YOUNG MAN: Marvin, I only said, "if." My father's Hungarian, my mother's Irish. Sorry, no Italian. Can I have the sip now?

MARVIN: Only if you tell me your *first* name.

YOUNG MAN: Marvin! Did I insist on getting your *last* name?

MARVIN: No, but this is different. I want to know.

YOUNG MAN: Oh! That *is* different. But I should warn you, you're not gonna like it any better than "God." You sure I can't have the sip first?

MARVIN: Positive. Out with the name.

YOUNG MAN (*sighs*): It's Yahweh.

MARVIN (*checks to be sure Bartender is out of earshot and lowers his voice*): You're really not kidding?

YOUNG MAN: Nope.

MARVIN: That's actually your name?

YOUNG MAN: Yup.

MARVIN (*shakes his head*): "Yahweh God" . . . I can't believe it.

YOUNG MAN: Sorry. It's the best I can do. (*Bartender leaves again.*)

MARVIN: Why on earth would your folks give you a name like that?

YOUNG MAN: You sure you wanna know?

MARVIN: Yeah. Tell me.

YOUNG MAN: Well . . . because that's who I am.

MARVIN (*looks around anxiously for Bartender*): Henry . . . Hey! Where'd he go?

YOUNG MAN: To the john again. His doctor's got him on diuretics.

MARVIN (*laughs nervously*): Heh, heh. So you're God, eh? (*He moves his stool back a little.*) Tell me, how do you like the work?

YOUNG MAN: I know this is hard for you, Marvin, but do me a favor and don't condescend. The job is tough enough.

MARVIN: But . . . but . . . Okay, listen. I'll tell you what I really think. If you're not just fooling around, then you definitely should be in therapy. I mean . . . for your own good.

YOUNG MAN: Why?

MARVIN: Well . . . lots of people think they're God, but with a little help, they get over it. I know a terrific doctor . . .

YOUNG MAN: Thanks, Marvin, but I'm afraid the treatment wouldn't work in my case.

MARVIN: Why not?

YOUNG MAN: The others get over it because they're not God.

MARVIN (*thinks carefully*): Okay. So you really believe you're God . . .

YOUNG MAN: No. I don't believe it, I *know* it. Would you say you only *believed* you were Marvin?

MARVIN: All right, all right. So you *think* you're God . . .

YOUNG MAN: No again. Same reasoning.

MARVIN: But listen. *Anybody* could say what you're saying . . .

YOUNG MAN: In the first place, Marvin, you know perfectly well almost nobody says it. And in the second, even if a million people did, that still doesn't make it crazy for God to say it.

MARVIN: If he exists, of course.

YOUNG MAN: Of course.

MARVIN: Damn right! So suppose I say there is no God . . .

YOUNG MAN: You mean, like, God is a metaphysical impossibility, therefore nobody can claim to be God?

MARVIN: Yeah, sort of.

YOUNG MAN: How come I didn't do that number on you when you said you were Marvin?

MARVIN: This is different.

YOUNG MAN: For you maybe, but not for me. You think it feels good when somebody I just met tells me I can't be who I say I am?

MARVIN: No, but . . .

YOUNG MAN: But what? Just because I'm God, you're excused from manners?

MARVIN: Well, no . . . (*He pounds the bar.*) But dammit, you *can't* be God!

YOUNG MAN (*shrugs*): Then you can't be Marvin.

MARVIN: But I *am!*

YOUNG MAN: Nope. You're an impostor. Give me back the Ballantine's.

MARVIN: I'm not an impostor! I really am Marvin.

YOUNG MAN: Okay. So keep the drink and stop giving me a hard time.

MARVIN: This is insane. We're getting nowhere.

YOUNG MAN: I was just about to mention that.

MARVIN: All right . . . (*He thinks.*) . . . Go back to where you said you didn't question my existence when I said I was Marvin . . .

YOUNG MAN: Can I interrupt?

MARVIN: Sure. What?

YOUNG MAN: Be accurate, Marvin. I never mentioned your *existence.* What I said I didn't question was your *identity.*

MARVIN: Okay, okay. My point is that Marvin is the name of a human being . . .

YOUNG MAN: Could be a dog.

MARVIN: Let me finish. So, when a human being comes up to you and says he's Marvin, you're not automatically suspicious . . .

YOUNG MAN: What if the dog said it?

MARVIN: Dogs can't talk.

YOUNG MAN: How about if a parrot?

MARVIN: That's different. It would be only a bird.

YOUNG MAN: But a parrot could be a Marvin, couldn't he?

MARVIN: Sure, but . . .

YOUNG MAN: But what? As a matter of fact, I'd trust a parrot over a human being any day when it came to giving me his right name. But you were saying?

MARVIN: You made me lose my point.

YOUNG MAN: No I didn't. All you were trying to say is that since a lot of Marvins are human beings, one more human being saying he's Marvin doesn't give you the willies: but that since God . . . go ahead and finish the sentence.

MARVIN (*brightening*): Ah! I've got it. . . . since God can't be a human being, then when a human being tells you he's God, you know something's fishy. There! What do you say to that?

YOUNG MAN: Who told you God can't be human?

MARVIN: Everybody knows that.

YOUNG MAN: Suppose nobody told God, though? If he decides he wants to be, you gonna tell him he's not allowed?

MARVIN: No, but . . .

YOUNG MAN: Look Marvin. The only thing God *can't* be is *not God.* Outside of that, it's an open ballgame. He could be a duck if he wanted.

MARVIN: You're telling me God is a duck, too?

YOUNG MAN: No, Marvin. I never had to go that far. It's only human beings who mess things up.

MARVIN: Okay, okay. Let me see if I can make any sense out of it. You're really God: suppose I give you that. But then doesn't that mean you can't be really human?

YOUNG MAN: You're worse than a mother, Marvin. First I can't be God. Now I can't be human. I suppose there's no use even *asking* if I can go out on a school night.

MARVIN: C'mon. You know what I'm getting at: the humanity's got to be just a disguise, right?

YOUNG MAN: What do you mean "just"? Even if it was a disguise, it would still have to be real: go to a party in a nonexistent mask and see how many people you fool. But in fact, it isn't a disguise. The point of a disguise is to keep you from finding out who's talking to you. Since I already blew my cover, the word doesn't apply.

MARVIN: What word do I want then?

YOUNG MAN: You wanna try "manifestation"?

MARVIN: You mean like "appearance"?

YOUNG MAN: No, Marvin, not like an appearance; more like a *communication*. An appearance only works if you know what the guy who's gonna show up actually looks like. But since nobody knows that about God, there's no such thing as an appearance of him. In a *communication*, though, all you have to do is trust that whoever's talking to you is really who he says, and you're home free.

MARVIN: So you're asking me to trust that you're both God and human at the same time?

YOUNG MAN: Right.

MARVIN: And that you're communicating with me . . .

YOUNG MAN: Right. But be accurate again: I'm communicating with you in a human way.

MARVIN: That's just a quibble.

YOUNG MAN: Believe me. It's not.

MARVIN: Anyway, what I had in mind was, since you're here, maybe you could tell me . . . I have a chance to buy into this condo in Fort Lauderdale: should I take it?

YOUNG MAN: Beats me.

MARVIN: What do you mean? I thought you said I should trust I was talking to God?

YOUNG MAN: You are. But also to a human being who never happened to be in real estate.

MARVIN: What's that got to do with it? God is supposed to know everything.

YOUNG MAN: And human beings are not. So when God communicates through a human being, he can't use all his moves.

MARVIN: Why?

YOUNG MAN: Marvin! Think! If he did, it would turn whoever he communicated through into a freak. People would only try to make a buck off him. Like you just did.

MARVIN: Sorry. No offense.

YOUNG MAN: Forget it. Why don't we get off this subject? Tell me. What do you do for a living?

MARVIN: I'm in women's wear. (*He giggles.*)

YOUNG MAN: That's funny?

MARVIN: No. It's just that I suddenly thought of something you could say if I asked you the same question. (*He laughs hard, pulling a handkerchief out of his pocket.*) "I work on the universe all week with only Saturdays off. What's worse, I have nobody I can say 'Thank God it's Friday' to."

YOUNG MAN: The only thing that's worse than God jokes, Marvin, is midget jokes. You want to hear what I actually do?

MARVIN (*puts handkerchief away*): You mean here in Cleveland? Sure.

YOUNG MAN: I cook. Six days a week. Tuesdays off.

MARVIN: Whereabouts?

YOUNG MAN: A place called Ristorante Piemontese. Northern Italian.

MARVIN: No kidding! I've eaten there. Some food! That's really you?

YOUNG MAN: Yeah, that's me in the back, loading on the butter and cream.

MARVIN: I know, I know. Cholesterol City. Tell me though. How'd you get into cooking?

YOUNG MAN: I sort of drifted in. I took business administration in community college for a while, but I couldn't stand accounting, so I quit and went to cooking school. I've been out three years.

MARVIN: That's all you do?

YOUNG MAN: What do you mean *all*? Anybody cooks for a living earns his money.

MARVIN: I didn't mean that. It's just that if you're really God, shouldn't you be doing something more . . . *religious*?

YOUNG MAN: Never appealed to me. As God, it wouldn't make sense: it'd be like expecting a horse trainer to go around wearing a bit in his mouth. And as a human being, frankly I didn't like religion any better than accounting.

MARVIN: But then, why are you here? You must have some kind of plan for fixing up the world. Or are you just going to cook veal scallopine forever and let it go at that?

YOUNG MAN: No, Marvin, I've got a plan; but since I'm human it couldn't involve cooking forever, even if I wanted it to. Fifty years maybe, tops. Still, though, cooking is as good a trade as any for what I have in mind.

MARVIN: You gonna tell me what that is?

YOUNG MAN: You really want to know?

MARVIN: Sure. Why not?

YOUNG MAN: You didn't like my name when you got it.

MARVIN: So?

YOUNG MAN: You're going to like this even less.

MARVIN: Still, try me.

YOUNG MAN: I'm going to fix the world up by dying and rising.

MARVIN (*shakes his head*): You were right. Even your name made more sense. How's that going to help? One guy dies and rises . . . unless he's got tremendous coverage, who'll even know about it? Maybe you should do it on prime time TV.

YOUNG MAN: I don't think so, Marvin. I haven't figured out all the details yet, but I've definitely ruled out a lot of coverage. Why do you think I'm in Cleveland?

MARVIN: But I'd have thought you'd want people to see it.

YOUNG MAN: That's not the important thing. When people see something, right away they figure it's outside themselves. What I want is that they should believe this is something *inside* themselves.

MARVIN: What? You mean the rising?

YOUNG MAN: Sure. When I rise, everybody does. Right then and there. They get a new life, even if they can't see it.

MARVIN: Oh. I kind of pictured you raising them individually.

YOUNG MAN: What do you want? I should schlep all over the country with a magic wand, doing people as if they were piecework? It would be a drag, Marvin. All at once has got more class.

MARVIN: But if they can't see anything happening to them, how will they know about it?

YOUNG MAN: Well, I've got two ideas on that. One is that it's not a matter of life and death for them just to know about it, because the new life is going to happen to them anyway. But the second is, they can always find out by being told how it happened to me.

MARVIN: But who's going to tell them? You?

YOUNG MAN: Probably not. The way I see it now, I'll probably just rise kind of privately, make sure a few dependable types have got the story straight, and then clear out.

MARVIN: Clear out?

YOUNG MAN: Only from the local scene, of course. But why shouldn't I? If I do the job once and for all, what's the point of hanging around in Cleveland?

MARVIN: Okay, okay. But what do you mean, dependable types?

YOUNG MAN: Witnesses, Marvin. People who can swear they saw me dead and then alive. I've got a few in mind. The only thing I haven't figured out is what kind of death I'll have.

MARVIN: Wouldn't it have to be something spectacular?

YOUNG MAN: What do you mean? Like skydiving without a parachute? Nah. That's too misleading. If you overdramatize the dying, people will start thinking they can't rise unless they have a fancy death, too. I almost think it would be best if mine was sort of . . . obscure.

MARVIN: You mean, like dying in bed of old age?

YOUNG MAN: That's a possibility; but every time I pray about it, I get negative vibrations. Probably won't happen that way.

MARVIN: You pray? I thought you were already God!

YOUNG MAN: Look, Marvin. Praying is how human beings get in touch with God. I'm human, so why should I be an exception? What do you want? Just because I happen to be also God, I should mess up my human head with a special trapdoor for in-house communications?

MARVIN: No, but . . .

YOUNG MAN: But nothing. It'd just make me another kind of freak.

MARVIN: Okay. Forget that. Go back to what kind of death. If it's not going to be in bed, how then?

YOUNG MAN: Well, as I said, I keep getting these negative vibes. Like maybe it'll be something violent. For a while there I tried to figure it in terms of work. You know, like the french fryer blowing up, or being locked accidentally in the walk-in freezer.

MARVIN: Which did you decide?

YOUNG MAN: Neither. I'm beginning to think maybe it won't be so impersonal.

MARVIN: How do you mean?

YOUNG MAN: Well, I notice something about myself. The clearer I get in my own mind about being God and dying and rising, the more I notice that other people very easily get pissed off at me. I mean, you were one of the nicer ones, Marvin. All you suggested was therapy. You should hear some of the things the religious types tell me to do.

MARVIN: I was only trying to help. You worried me.

YOUNG MAN: Believe me, I appreciate it. But as I was saying. I'm beginning to think maybe the way I'll die will be decided by other people. You know. Like getting on my case and accusing me of a capital crime or something.

MARVIN: You don't think maybe they'll just form a lynch mob?

YOUNG MAN: I had that idea for a while, but now I don't think so. More likely, it'll be something legal.

MARVIN: You mean, capital punishment? Isn't that practically un-constitutional unless you shoot a cop?

YOUNG MAN: Practically is not absolutely, Marvin. Look at the way the Supreme Court has been going since Nixon. You can sit there and tell me you think capital punishment is on the way out?

MARVIN: But what could they give you the death penalty for? I mean . . . after all, you're God. You wouldn't commit a murder just to arrange it, would you?

YOUNG MAN: Of course not. But they could still nail me for something I didn't mean to do, couldn't they?

MARVIN: How?

YOUNG MAN: Oh I don't know. Suppose I get mixed up with this girl who's just stringing me along because what she really wants is to dump her husband for some Mafia lover. But the husband is religious and won't give her a divorce. So she and her lover have it all set up: I'm in the bedroom with her, and her husband comes in, and she hands me a gun and says it's a burglar, and with one thing and another I shoot him. Then she turns on me and swears I was forcing her and all that, like in a novel . . . you know what I mean?

MARVIN: Yeah. But it wouldn't work. For one thing, when the Mafia wants somebody dead, they don't hire a cook who thinks he's a novelist. But for another, that bedroom stuff doesn't exactly square with the God business.

YOUNG MAN: I know what you mean. But you know something? I tried a long time to figure out a nice respectable death for my-self, but I finally gave up on it. After all, the only thing I really need to rise is to be dead. Everything else is strictly secondary.

MARVIN: But you don't think it should at least be a little . . . moral? For the sake of giving a good example?

YOUNG MAN: Nah, Marvin. I worked my way through that one too. First of all, I thought, how many people have I met who are actually looking for an example of how to die? How to live maybe—or more likely, how to earn a buck or make out. But not to die. Second, I asked myself, if I'm gonna go through death for everybody, why should I be so fussy it should be a moral death? I mean, there's gotta be a good twenty, maybe thirty percent of the world's population whose deaths are distinctly crummy from an ethical point of view. Why should I make such people feel miserable?

MARVIN: You mean, you're going to raise bad people too?

YOUNG MAN: Sure. But don't get me onto that now. Finally, I said to myself, if thirty percent of all deaths are unethical, there's gotta be something like forty or fifty percent that are just mindless. Like for instance, being blown up by a land mine, or dying in a hospital with a flat EEG. Why should I worry about whether my death will have a lot of nice moral shadings to it? A good half of the people I raise would have died in no position to think about such things.

MARVIN: I must say, for God you got a pretty loose outlook.

YOUNG MAN: I got that because I'm God, Marvin. Morality is all right as far as it goes, but it's got two big drawbacks. One is that as a way of helping the world get its act together it stinks, because the number of truly moral people is so close to zero it'd make you cry. But the second thing is that when all the semi-moral types start cheering for morality, you better duck. Ninety-nine percent of the time they end up using it like a stick to beat up on somebody.

MARVIN: Boy, is that ever true. You know? I've got a hunch it could be them and not the religious types who do you in.

YOUNG MAN: That's a good point, Marvin. I must say, you catch on pretty quick. You wouldn't like to be one of the witnesses would you?

MARVIN: You mean, right now? I can't. I've got a plane to make in an hour.

YOUNG MAN: No, not now. Maybe in a couple of years though. You get to Cleveland a lot?

MARVIN (*cagily*): Sometimes. Why?

YOUNG MAN: We could get together more. How often do you fly in?

MARVIN: Well . . . (*He looks embarrassed.*) Oh hell! What have I got to hide? I'm here every Thursday overnight. There's this girl . . . my wife thinks I'm on business and sometimes I am. But if I sold as much as I told her these past two years, Cleveland would be up to its eyebrows in country casuals.

YOUNG MAN: What's the girl's name?

MARVIN: Jennifer.

YOUNG MAN: Is she nice?

MARVIN: Very. Who knows? Maybe someday . . . but I suppose that all disqualifies me as a witness, huh?

YOUNG MAN: Marvin! You disappoint me. Why should I get fussy all of sudden? You know dead when you see it, don't you?

MARVIN: Well, sure.

YOUNG MAN: And you'd probably recognize risen, too, wouldn't you?

MARVIN: I guess.

YOUNG MAN: So what's the problem? It can't be lack of enthusiasm. Anybody gets to Cleveland once a week for two years has got to have a lot of staying power. Also, you've got a nice sense of concern. How about it?

MARVIN (*thinks*): Could I give you a maybe?

YOUNG MAN: How do you mean?

MARVIN: Well. Suppose next week I miss the red-eye flight again? I could meet you Friday morning, just like now.

YOUNG MAN: Yeah. I'd like that. I don't get off work till one anyway. If I stay on and do some prep, I'll be that much ahead. I'll see you then.

MARVIN: You've got a deal. (*Looks at his watch.*) I guess I better go though and see about a seat on the next flight. (*Picks up his suitcase and heads for door.*) See you in a week. (*At the door, he turns around, looks back and smiles.*) Hey! Maybe you thought I forgot, but you never did get your sip. I left you some in the glass. Enjoy!

YOUNG MAN: Marvin, you're a real prize. Thanks a lot. (*Turns to the Bartender.*) Well, Henry . . . it takes time, but it's worth it. Every now and then you actually run into a warm one.

1

Before I tell you what happened when I actually showed up in Cleveland a week later, let me introduce myself. My full name is Marvin H. Goodman, I'm forty-six years old, and as you know, I'm in the garment business. The middle initial? Never mind. The only thing it could possibly stand for at this point in the story is However.

The way I planned the trip, it was going to be just a nice visit with Jennifer Thursday night and then straight back to New York Friday on the red-eye connection from LA. So what, I told myself, if I'd promised to miss the plane on purpose and meet this cook character in the bar again at five in the morning? My life was already not a model of simplicity. Another conversation with a chef who claimed he was God, I didn't exactly need.

However . . . (my brother Howard, who's in real estate, says nobody ever heard a piece of good news that began with however) . . . there I was outside the same bar a week later, having missed the flight anyway.

At my age, I should know not to trust electric clocks. I even have this terrific digital watch Shirley gave me—with a computer and a beep alarm and probably six other things I haven't discovered yet—but when I'm in bed with Jennifer, I can never bring myself to wake us up with my wife's present. What do I get though, for not crossing personal wires? Half the power lines in Cleveland fall down that night in a storm.

However. After I get to the departure gate just in time to watch the L-1011 go blinking off into the dark, I say to myself, What the hell, there are worse ways to kill an hour; I'll go meet him anyway. And what do I find? The bar is closed, of course.

My howevers, however, always come in threes. There I am, banging on the roll-down steel front with my sample case, thinking I'm all alone, when this voice like something out of the Addams Family comes rumbling up behind me, "Easy, Marvin. Easy."

Well, the first thing is, I practically jump out of my skin. The second, naturally, is that I do a fast pivot to see what kind of monster it is that makes the world's lowest sound—and sure enough, it *is* Lurch. Or at least his kid brother: six feet, seven inches of twenty-eight year old dressed in a black suit and a white shirt. Also, I notice, no tie and white socks—which in my experience usually means a violinist, except this guy could hardly fit his hands on a bass fiddle.

It's funny how when you try not to act scared, all you can manage is to sound stupid. I mean, if a dog had been surprised like that by this giant, he would have come on snarling or something. But not me. A big deep voice tells Marvin to be cool, Marvin turns into a frozen pussycat. "Heh, heh," I say. "You know my name, huh? How come is that?"

"Jerry told me."

Now obviously, since I never knew a Jerry in my whole life, I have to assume he's referring to the chef I met last week. But, once you've been stupid, the only thing left is to be stubborn about it. So I ask him, "Who's Jerry?"

"My cousin."

"Your cousin, huh?" I say this with a little smile as if he's feebleminded—and then I round out a brilliant performance by being sarcastic: "I'm supposed to know your cousin? I don't even know you."

"Oh, I'm Spencer. Jerry sent me. He cut his thumb a few hours ago boning chicken legs and had to have some stitches. He says to say he's sorry and hopes you don't mind talking to me instead."

This is the first time I've gotten more than three words out of him, so I'm finally able to zero in on something about his voice other than that it sounds like the last note on the Radio City organ. He's got a southwestern drawl. Actually, it makes him come across more friendly and polite than he looks, but I'm not ready to give in yet, so I go back to sounding stupid. I consider a lot of options and then say "Oh."

Now it's his turn to be confused. "You *are* the right Marvin, aren't you? The one he had the talk with last Friday? I hope I haven't made a mistake."

Finally, the guy gets to me. He's really not much more than a big kid, so I decide to apologize. "No. Don't worry. I'm the right one. It's just . . . well, a lot of things. For one, I didn't really intend to show up here. For another, you scared me pretty good. For a third, he never did tell me his name."

"He didn't? Why, that's not like him at all. Normally, he's sociable to a fault."

"Oh, he was sociable enough. What I meant was, he never told me his name was Jerry. In fact, he spent most of the time trying to convince me it was something else."

"To convince you? Who on earth did he say he was?"

This Spencer is beginning to get my interest. He still sounds and looks weird—his eyes, as a matter of fact, look like two Ping-Pong balls with half-inch black holes straight through them. But he seems gentle enough—and he acts as if I know more about his cousin than he does. Since I find this hard to believe, I ask him "You really have no idea what he told me?"

He swears he doesn't, so I lay it out for him as if I heard this kind of thing every day. "Oh, Well. He said his name was God—his last name, that is. His first name was Yahweh."

I don't know what reaction I expected to a straight line like that—maybe a "No!" or an "Oh, dear me!" or maybe just a big hoot—but all I get is, "He actually said that?"

"What?" I say. "He doesn't do that all the time? He had it pretty well worked out as far as I could see."

Spencer went into a kind of funk. I couldn't tell if he was surprised, or miffed, or what, so when he didn't say anything, I just started babbling on like I usually do. "Listen. If we're gonna talk about this, there's no point standing here on one foot. Let's go someplace we can have at least a cup of coffee."

Right away, he starts walking off in the wrong direction. I'm not a short person, but I have to take two steps to his one even to get within ten feet of him. "Hey!" I yell, "The coffee shop's back the other way, down the corridor on the right." He reverses field without a word, and I follow him feeling like a bird dog. "Too bad that bar wasn't open, like last week."

"It was *open*?" he says, finally coming back from wherever he went in his head. "Jerry never mentioned he'd talked to you *in* the bar—only that I should meet you outside it." He shook his head.

Now that I thought about it, I wondered too. "Well," I say, "it's just one more piece that doesn't fit. Believe me, the whole experience was pretty weird. But then he's your cousin. I guess you're used to him."

Spencer puts on what I suppose is meant to be a half smile, but it takes so much work it gets only to about a tenth. "People don't exactly get used to Jerry. To tell you the truth, I never heard any of this before. But then, he's always trying different things on for size, so to speak. You just never know with him."

This makes me really wonder. "Look," I say. "I don't want to sound nosy or anything, but is he really . . . you know . . . all right?"

"Oh shucks, yes. It was only five stitches. He'll be back at work by noon. I declare. You *are* a thoughtful person, just like he said."

This strikes me as so far off the wall, I just ignore it. "Hey, here's the coffee shop. C'mon. I'll buy."

We go in and sit down in a booth at the back. When the waitress comes, she plops the menus on the table like a couple of fish and stands there with her arms folded, tapping her foot. I realize this place is not the Four Seasons and that maybe she had a bad night, but still, I'm a little annoyed. So I hand my menu back and tell her, "Never mind. All I need is coffee and an apricot danish." When I look over though to ask Spencer what he wants, I see he's already eating some kind of sawdust out of a brown paper bag. "Nothing for me, thank you," he says handing his menu back

too. "What I have here will do me just fine." She gives us both an
expert shrug and farches off. ("Farch" is one of my brother Howie's
words: it's a combination of flippancy and marching.)

Anyway, I say to Spencer, "Listen. You sure you don't want a
little something more substantial?" He's got his mouth full though,
so he just shakes his head. While he's swallowing, I decide to be
funny. "Heh, heh. You know, that stuff looks bad enough to be
good for you. What is it?"

"It's gorp," he says. "Would you like some?"

"What's in it?"

"Dried fruit, nuts and seeds. No sulphur, no sugar." He pushes
the bag over, but I tell him, "If it's all the same, I'll stick with the
coffee and danish."

He shakes his head like I'm making some terrible mistake.
"Caffeine, animal fat and refined sugar," he says. "Just the thought
of it makes my whole body feel threatened."

"If it would make you feel better, I could change to a toasted
english."

"No," he says. "That just adds BHA and BHT. Go ahead and
have what you like. It's your cardiovascular system."

I've met my share of food nuts—or, when they're like Spencer,
I guess I should say nut nuts. It's almost impossible to get them
off the subject, so I try to get him at least off my case. "That's
interesting," I say. "You and your cousin ever discuss food? I mean,
the stuff he cooks at that restaurant, talk about a threat! Or maybe
he doesn't eat it, huh?"

Spencer actually shudders. "He eats it," he says, as if he's talking about somebody swallowing live mice. "But that's only one of
the problems I have with him. Tell me something. When he was
talking to you about being God and all . . . I know this may be hard
for you to judge, but if I told you that in recent years most people
have found him extremely laid-back, would you say that still fits?
Or did he sound . . . more serious?"

Spencer sat back and munched another handful of gorp. I
didn't know what to say, but I was beginning to get a funny feeling. I hardly know this Jerry, and now I'm suddenly being treated

like an expert on him by his own cousin. Still, it was better than
sitting through a sales pitch for vegetarianism. Just to keep up his
interest, I tell him, "Yes to both."

At this point, the waitress comes with my danish and—like
I could have told before I even looked—with *two* coffees. One
thing I hate is hassling the help in restaurants. It always strikes me
as pushy, even when, like this girl, they're the kind a good shove
wouldn't hurt a bit. So without giving Spencer even time to think
about sending it back, I say to her, "Don't worry about the extra
coffee. I like mine cold anyway; it can be my second cup." The
shrug she gives us this time is definitely world-class. When she's
gone, he asks me what I meant by "Yes to both."

"Well," I say, "the only people I ever met who were more laid-
back than he was were asleep, so I guess the first answer is he hasn't
changed much at all. On the other hand, I'd have to say he definitely seemed serious. He talked a lot about dying . . ." (I knew the
next part sounded wild even before I got it out, but I figured what
the hell, play it straight) . . . "and, of course, about rising also."

"He actually talked about that? Doing a *miracle*, I mean?"

"It's hard to tell. The way I just said it, it sounds pretty miraculous, I admit. But when he talked about it, it came across as sort
of ordinary."

"*Ordinary?*"

"Yeah. According to him, when he rises, everybody else does
too. Only the catch is they don't particularly know about it. They
can only believe it."

"Shee-it," Spencer says. "More of the same."

His reaction is a mystery to me. But since this part of Jerry's
pitch was even more of a mystery, I just take a guess: "What's the
problem? He's talking through his hat?"

"Oh, no. It's not that . . ."

"What then? Don't tell me you think he can actually do such
a thing. Come back from the dead, I mean. You really believe he
has miraculous powers?"

"I've never questioned that about him. My problem is the way
he seems to be using them nowadays."

At this point, I draw a complete blank, so I say, "Look, Spencer. Maybe you should talk and I'll listen. Your cousin got me so confused last week, I decided not to bother looking him up again. So what happens? Today, by pure accident, I meet you and get even more confused."

"It wasn't an accident."

I want to say, come on now, but I restrain myself and settle for "What was it then?"

"It was another one of those laid-back, unrecognizable miracles of his."

I suppose this means the power failure, but it strikes me as so far-fetched, all I can say is, "*Another* one?"

"Yes. Like the bar being open last Friday at five a.m. and God knows what all else. He always insists on making his miracles look like accidents—so people don't get the wrong idea, he says. But if you ask me, that only gives them no idea whatsoever."

O . . . kay, Spencer, I think to myself. Whatever you say. Only now you're gonna have to clue me in a lot better than you've been doing. So I look him straight in the Ping-Pong-ball eyes and I say, "Hey, do me one favor. If there's a beginning to all this, maybe please you could go back and start there? You've got me totally lost."

"I'm afraid it's a long story."

"Don't worry. I interrupt a lot."

"It goes all the way back to our mothers—Jerry's and mine, that is."

"Don't apologize. More of a beginning I couldn't ask for. What about them?"

"Well, they were—in fact, they still are—both involved in psychic phenomena."

"What? Fortune telling? Ouija boards? Making things float in the air?"

"All of it. ESP, telekinesis, numerology, astrology. Plus Tarot cards, the I Ching and Tai Chi. We were practically weaned on things like that. But to keep the story short, they had Jerry and me just six months apart and somehow they decided it all meant that he and I would get together when we were around thirty for a really important project . . ."

"Your mothers knew each other back then?"

"Yes. They're the real cousins. We're just second or third—I can never remember which."

"Don't let it stop you. The key word was 'important project.' What was it supposed to be? Something like fixing up the whole world?"

"As a matter of fact, yes. How did you know?"

"From Jerry. Your mothers told you about this when you were little kids?"

"Not exactly. That came later on. When we were small, we only knew we had these special powers."

One thing about me. When I'm busy helping somebody along with a story, I don't always take in right away what he's saying. But now, suddenly I'm aware he's including himself in the power business.

"Er, Spencer. Just a minute. I notice you said 'we.' You have this ability to . . . to *arrange* things also?"

"Yes."

"I mean, you can do . . . miracles?"

"Yes."

"You're not God too, are you?"

"No. Of course not."

It's funny how relative things are. Two weeks ago, if I met somebody who claimed to be a miracle worker, I'd have been all over him with skepticism; here I am, actually relieved that's all he is. "Oh, good," I say. "You really do have powers, though? I mean . . . that you could show me? Like now?"

"Did you ask Jerry that?"

"Sort of."

"What did you want him to do?"

"I asked him a simple real estate question anybody who reads the *Times* could probably answer. I figured for God it'd be a snap."

"But he begged off, didn't he?" Spencer shook his head. "I declare. I just can't understand his reluctance."

"You mean, *you* would be willing to do a . . . well, I realize calling it a demonstration makes it sound like a pitch for Electrolux or something, but you know what I mean."

He took a deep breath and looked kind of sad. "Look," I said. "If it's too much trouble, I can take a rain check."

"No," he sighed. "May I borrow your watch?"

"Sure. But you'll be careful, huh? It's got a computer built right into it. I hate to think what it'd cost if I had to have it fixed."

He took it from me and sort of checked out the computer buttons for awhile. Then he looked up and said, "Would you like to talk to your wife and tell her you missed your flight?"

"What? You mean now? On the watch?"

"No. On the pay phone over there by the door. I'll just use the watch to get in touch with her."

I hadn't exactly been thinking of Shirley, even though it was her present. I guess what with that and Jennifer and everything, I hesitated one beat too long.

"Don't you *want* to talk to her?"

"Well, now that you mention it, she's probably asleep. It might upset her."

"Who would you like to speak with then? Do you have a brother? Or a partner?"

This isn't so good either. My brother, I made the mistake of telling about Jennifer. He's a big family man so he doesn't exactly approve how much time I spend in Cleveland. And my partner Irving is hardly a better idea. Since I haven't done even one phone call's worth of business on this trip, I'd just as soon not have to cook up something to tell him. I think fast. Irving normally catches the 6:30 out of Cold Spring Harbor, so I stretch it a little. "No, he gets a very early train. He's probably on his way already."

"Are you sure you want me to do this demonstration?"

Maybe I'm dense. Or maybe I'm just not the world's most critical person. But in any case, I don't make comparisons in a hurry. Now, though, I definitely feel one coming on. Spencer may have a problem with his cousin, but suddenly I'm having one with him. Last week, when I gave Jerry the little confession about my private life, he passed it off like a gentleman. This guy I've told absolutely nothing and he's making me feel guilty as hell.

"Oh yes," I tell him. "Definitely. It's just that I have to think who I could call at this hour. Hey! I've got it! How about the New York weather? It's 212-976-1616."

"Whatever you like, Marvin. It'll just be a little strange. I'm going to do this as an operator callback. What is your last name?"

I tell him "Goodman" and then start to say something funny about how Jerry tried for a whole hour to get that out of me. But he puts on an even sadder look, so I just shut up and stare while he punches buttons on the watch. After about twenty seconds, he says, "When the phone rings, it will be for you. You'd better go over now so no one else picks it up."

I have never felt so dumb in my whole life. I get up out of the booth, and while I'm walking toward the phone, it actually rings. I make an idiotic dash to pick it up and this voice says, "Mr. Goodman? We have your party on the line. Are you sure this is the number you wanted to reach?"

I honestly can't remember what I said, or even what the weather was. I just hung up and went back and collapsed in the booth. "That's incredible," I said when I caught my breath. "How'd you do it?"

"I'm afraid I can't tell you that."

"Why? It's a secret?"

"No. I don't understand exactly how I do it. I just know I can."

"But you've gotta know more about it than that."

"Not necessarily, Marvin. When something is really difficult, all your energy goes into the sheer doing of it. You don't have to get involved in figuring out how."

"That doesn't make any sense."

"Sure it does. Didn't you ever ask an artist how he does what he does—the whole, finished performance, I mean? He'll always tell you *that's* the question that makes no sense. The *what* is hard enough without worrying about the *how*."

"But I always thought miracles were supposed to be sort of . . . easy. You know. Prang! And they're done."

"That's only because you never talked to anyone who did them before."

"You mean it's actually work?" I ask the question just because I'm babbling along, but then I take a good look at his face and feel funny about it. He's absolutely exhausted.

"I'm afraid it is," he said, giving his face a dry wash with his hands.

"I'm sorry. I shouldn't have asked."

"Oh, that's all right. It's just that miracles make me sleepy. I guess I'm lucky not to be like Jerry, though. I've only seen him do a couple, but he gets almost impossibly angry every time."

"*Angry?*"

"Yes. I guess they affect different people different ways. He says that's why he refuses to do them, but I can't believe that's the real reason. I simply don't know what to think about him."

This is the second time he's said that, so just to get him going again, I ask what it is exactly that bothers him so much about Jerry.

"Well. You remember I told you about our mothers' deciding he and I would end up working together on something big?"

"Sure. Fixing up the world, right?"

"Right. But what I didn't tell you was that he was supposed to be the really important person. My part was only to kind of get things ready for him."

"I see," I tell him, trying to sound bright. Actually, I'm completely in the dark, but I can't think of anything better to say.

"While we were kids growing up, it didn't seem like much of a problem. I mean, we'd sit around talking about all the ways the world was going straight to hell—you know, wars, and the military-industrial complex, and pollution, and the loss of contact with the soil—and we were fairly agreed as to what ought to be done about it."

"You talked a lot? Funny, you and he sound like you grew up in different parts of the country. I'm good at accents. He's definitely New York, with a little Cleveland on the side. But you? I'd have to say you were North Texas, maybe."

"That's very perceptive of you, Marvin. We were both born in

New York; but my folks were from the south and couldn't stand the winters, so they moved when I was very, very young. We actually lived in Texarkana for awhile, just like you said. Most of my boyhood, though, was spent in Tulsa."

He was wandering, so I nudged him back on the track again. "Still, you and Jerry managed to talk a lot? How was that?"

"Oh. Most every year we'd spend the whole summer together."

"Fair enough. So the two of you talked about the world. Tell me, what did you decide you were going to do?"

"Well, we came up with all the usual things, I suppose. Antiwar demonstrations, anti-nuclear protests, back-to-the-land movements, no exploitation of the environment, social justice, encouraging people to purge their bodies of the poisons of affluence, development of the inner self, meditation . . ."

"Jerry was into that stuff, too? I must say, from my conversation with him, I'd never have guessed it."

"That's precisely my problem. The nearer we get to the time we're supposed to do something, the further apart we seem to be on the program. Why, I actually went so far as to move here to Cleveland a year ago—just so we could be closer, you know—and would you believe, I don't think I've spent more than twenty-four hours with him in the whole time."

I never like listening to complaints about people. Right away, I feel I have to make excuses for them. "Maybe he's just busy. A chef has a six-day week at least."

"It's not just the time, Marvin. It's the way he's been drifting. He just doesn't seem to have his old zeal for the right things."

Spencer goes quiet for a couple of seconds, then all of a sudden, his eyes pop wide open and he gets wound up. "Why, I remember one day—I think it was back in '71 or '72—he actually went and messed up the Selective Service records of the entire city of Cleveland. Shee-it! You should've seen it. *That* was a *miracle!*"

"It was good, huh?"

"It was terrific! He took this toy walkie-talkie and just stood outside the Draft Board office on the sidewalk. Then he put everything he had into it and pushed the button. Glory be! He burned out every circuit in the computer. There was smoke pouring out the windows, and people running all over the place—they never did figure out what hit them. Took six months to get it all back together."

Spencer had tears running down his cheeks, he was so excited. Still, demonstrations are not my style, so I try to get him off the subject. "What about Jerry? He got angry that time too?"

"Did he ever! He wasn't fit to talk to for a week. Swore he'd never do anything like that again."

"And did he?"

"No. Unfortunately." Since Spencer's face drops almost lower than his voice when he says this, I think maybe I can finally put my finger on what's bothering him: "So that's your problem, huh? He won't do miracles anymore."

"No, Marvin. That's still only part of it. I could see his argument that protests like that don't produce much lasting benefit. What I couldn't see was the way he started backing away from all the other good things we agreed on."

This time, I can almost smell the lecture coming on brown rice and honey with pieces of wax in it. I decide to do an end run around his cousin's connection with veal, butter and cream. "You mean, like *meditation* or something? I don't think you have any worries. Jerry made a point of telling me he prays."

"But what did he mean by that, Marvin? You know what he told *me* he does when he prays? He asks for *answers!*"

Spencer says this with a lot of force, so even though it doesn't seem like such a horrible idea to me, I go along with him. "That's bad, huh?"

"Of course it is, Marvin. The purpose of meditation is to eliminate everything that disturbs a person's *Wa*—to reach a state of complete acceptance of *karma*. Asking for anything simply sets you at odds with the universe."

As I said, I'm slow to make comparisons. But now another one begins to dawn on me: in spite of the God business, Jerry is suddenly looking pretty good again. I mean, he at least sounds like somebody a regular person could spend an evening with. Between

Spencer's bag of seeds and his *Wa*, I'd be up the wall in an hour.
Still, who am I to be critical? I ask him, "What's a *Wa*?"

"Harmony, Marvin. Harmony. It's there for everyone, if only
they'll eliminate the things that disturb it."

"In my experience, that could be one hell of a lot of things."
This, I realize, is coming on stronger than I meant to, but then . . .

"Look, Spencer," I say to him. "You ever think possibly this
harmony business of yours might have just a little hot air in it? I'm
no psychologist, but maybe if you didn't make such a big deal about
your *Wa*, your cousin wouldn't be so much of a problem."

"What do you mean?"

"I mean that there's no way somebody like Jerry—somebody
who claims he's really God, that is—is not gonna disturb the hell
out of everybody."

"But I'd be perfectly willing to believe he was God . . ."

"No you wouldn't, Spencer. You'd only believe him if he swore
off what you consider ungodly things. Which is not exactly trusting
somebody, you know. It's more like asking him to pass a test."

"But the ungodly things—he agreed to swear off them once
himself."

"Spencer! He was a kid then . . ." As I start to say this, the
waitress comes by without even stopping and drops the check, so I
hold up a finger to interrupt myself and pretend I'm figuring the tip
I'm not giving her. I need a minute to think. What am I doing here,
arguing for things I already said I didn't believe? I decide to stand
up and put on my coat before something even funnier happens.

Spencer gets up too, but he's not about to let me go. "How
does his being a kid enter into it if he's really been God all along?"

"What?" I say to him. "Just because he's God, he can't get rid
of a dim idea when he outgrows it?" Suddenly for some reason, I
hear myself. Holy shit, I think. I'm beginning to sound exactly like
Jerry.

We head for the cash register, but Spencer still can't get off the
subject. "Those things weren't all dim ideas."

"Who's to say? Maybe he's just seen brighter ones."

"I really would like to believe that, you know."

"Yeah, I guess. But you never will if you keep wishing he was back munching vegetables and blowing up computers. Look, I talked to him. As far as I can see, he's not going that way. If he's the important one, you just have to trust *him*, period."

"You mean, with no ideal criteria involved at all?"

"You got it, Spencer. Take me, for instance. I'm one up on you . . . as a matter of fact, make that two. First, I think his laid-back attitude is absolutely terrific, so I haven't got your problems with it. But second, he's also clued me in on the dying and rising business—which apparently you never even heard of . . ."

"But do you think it was *right* for him not to tell me something as import . . ."

"Spencer, don't interrupt." I give the cashier my money and turn back to him. "All I'm saying is that even though I'm two ahead of you, trusting him means trusting *him*, not just the things I happen to like about him. For all I know, in a couple of weeks he could come around completely changed—like no more Mr. Laid Back, maybe, or with the idea of rising from the dead dumped in the trash can for good—whatever. The point is, if I want to go along with him, what's got to count is what *he* says, whenever he says it—not a bunch of stuff I turned into my own pet ideas."

Spencer stood there and rubbed his chin while I picked up my change. "You know?" he said. "I never thought of it that way. You really *do* trust him, don't you?"

"I didn't till you talked me into it, Spencer. Tell Jerry I'll see him next Friday."

2

As things worked out, I did see Jerry that next week—and I kept on seeing him maybe twice a month over the next couple of years. If you don't mind though, I'd just as soon not spend a whole lot of time rehashing that part of my life.

For one thing, nothing much actually happened as far as Jerry was concerned. He worked right along at his job but otherwise stayed out of sight. Mostly, I would see him at the restaurant. Jennifer and I got into the habit of going there on Thursdays and after a couple of meals I introduced them. She liked him right away.

Sometimes, when he wasn't so busy, we'd go back in the kitchen and just talk. Spencer was right. Jerry always was trying different ideas on for size. I should get credit though, for being psychic. You remember I said maybe he'd come back in a couple of weeks with a completely different pitch? Well he did. And I hit it right on the head.

All the God business—plus the dying and rising, too—went straight out the window. Not that he reneged on it. He just never got on the subject anymore. What he was into now was a complicated thing about making a New Order in the world. As a matter of fact, he began to sound a lot like Spencer, except he never, thank God, carried on about his *Wa*.

Which reminds me I should tell you about Spencer. He went public with a vengeance. I'd never have guessed it just talking to him one on one, but in front of a crowd he was a regular Billy Graham. He actually got a movement going. What he'd do was collect these huge crowds at a place down on Lake Erie and then lay

into them about renouncing the Old Order and all its poisons—
which, as you can imagine, included just about everything except
bird food. Funny, though, a lot of people bought it. Kids especially.

I was even slightly involved myself. He worked out an initiation ceremony which he'd hold at the end of every rally—a kind
of sawdust trail thing in which everybody who wanted to do a lot
of renouncing would come forward and receive three things. The
first was a new white sweatshirt, perfectly plain. The second was
a small white stone. And the third was what he called the New
Name for the New Order. Everybody who came up got a different
name, and only they themselves were supposed to know it. (It was
written on the stone in pencil and they had to rub it off before he'd
let them go.)

Anyway, my part in it was only at the beginning. One night,
a year ago last April, Spencer comes to see me. He says he has
this ritual he's getting up with sweatshirts and white stones, and
he wonders how he's gonna manage the shirts without any money.
He wants to know, since I'm in the garment business, can I help
him out?

I say, "Sure, probably," and even offer to let him have them on
consignment. I tell him he can sell them for a few cents over cost
and pay me back whenever. Ha! I should have known. Spencer
is also against markups. Not only that, He doesn't think much of
breaking even, either. They're gonna be giveaways, just like the
stones.

"Listen, Spencer," I tell him, "stones I can get you for free; case
lots of sweatshirts don't usually wash up on the beach." But like a
dope, I tell him I'll try, so he thanks me for both the shirts *and* the
stones and disappears into the night.

I got them for him: nice hooded numbers, 60 percent cotton,
40 percent acrylic—and made in Poland no less. Unfortunately,
plain white I could find only in XL, so on some of Spencer's size 5
converts they looked like nightshirts. Still, there were twelve cases
and I made him a present of the whole lot—plus the stones, which
I personally picked up on the north shore of Long Island.

Just so you don't think I'm some kind of fanatic or saint though,

I should set the record straight. For one thing, I never actually went through Spencer's ceremony myself. For another, the sweatshirts hardly cost me at all: items like that may not land on the beach, but they do sometimes fall off trucks. Not that I'd ever deal with the mob, of course. But if I just happen to know a friend who has them on, say, the second bounce after the truck . . . well, I figure 20 percent of the Gross National Product is pilfered, so it makes me at least one-fifth patriotic.

But to finish up about Jerry. As I said, he was into this New Order thing almost as much as Spencer. He even said that one of these days he'd actually go through the initiation ceremony himself. Still, he always kept a kind of distance between himself and his cousin. It's hard to put a finger on, but maybe the way to say it is that Spencer's version of the idea always seemed to call for mobs of people. You know. Like the New Order could come off only if absolutely everybody got into the act. When Jerry talked about it, he made it sound as if nobody besides himself would have to do a thing.

"Marvin, *think!*" he would say to me. "Spencer's a terrific person, but he's barking up a tree that isn't even there. To improve the world his way, he needs a hundred percent favorable response—not a one-point-five, which is the most he's gonna get. But even if he could hit ninety-nine, it'd still be no good. The New Order has to have *zero* monkey wrenches in the works, otherwise it turns right back into the same old heap we've got now. Nah, Marvin. My way is better. If I do it all myself, at least I'll know it's done."

As I said, he never got into the God talk anymore, but somehow he made himself sound more important without it. Jennifer noticed that right off. She said she was glad she never heard the Yahweh bit from him. This way, she said, a person only had to decide whether they would like it if Jerry could actually make the world better, not whether he could prove he was somebody they could never check up on anyway.

Which brings me, unfortunately, to the other reason I'm not all that eager to drag up the past two years: Jennifer.

I don't know exactly how to tell you this, so let me just wander into it my own way. When I first got to know her, she was a host-ess in a cocktail lounge: one of those hotel-basement Ye Olde Pub places, full of rust carpet, thick pine tables and lots of guys—some of whom gave you the feeling they were measuring you for a ce-ment kimono every time they looked at you. You know: very nice clothes, and very little else nice.

Well, anyway, when I met her she was involved with this type who had Mafia written all over him in capitals. And what did Mar-vin do? Marvin moved right in, naturally. Again though, just so you don't think I'm a hero, I had no idea she was his steady, and I certainly didn't know his line of work. However, by sheer dumb luck, he happened to be ready to dump her anyway, so I didn't end up as part of the pollution in Lake Erie. Instead, Jennifer and I just hit it off from word one.

All I can tell you is, what came after that was the best time of my life. We were different ages, of course. I had a good nineteen years on her, but we sort of grew together—me down, and her up—till we both arrived at the same age. We used to tell each other we were thirty-three.

That's funny, you know. My brother Howie is a great kid-der. When somebody complains they don't feel good, he tells them they shouldn't expect to, except once in their lives. He says the only time a human being ever has absolutely nothing wrong with them—no heartaches, no hemorrhoids, no hangovers, no problems at all—is for one hour early on a Wednesday morning sometime be-tween the ages of twenty-nine and thirty-three. Unfortunately, he says, most people sleep through it.

Well, I didn't. And it wasn't just one morning, either. In fact, I felt good for so long, I actually started to fall in love with Cleveland. Not to mention New York. You know all the sycamore trees in Manhattan? How on a winter afternoon, when the sun hits them, the bark turns this deep gold? Well, I used to tell Jennifer that every time I saw one I would send it to her right on the spot. She called me the golden logger. It sounds silly, I guess, but it wasn't. Nobody in the whole world ever had anything better.

I'm sorry. Look. Just so I don't stall out completely, let me tell

it to you straight: my not-so-simple life finally caught up with me.
Or, if that's not straight enough, Jennifer found out I was fooling
around on the side with somebody else in New York and slammed
the door in my face.

Now that I hear it, that sounds dumb, so I suppose I have to tell
you more. Actually, she didn't find out, she guessed. But the result
was, she started getting distant. And it wasn't just my imagination:
she waved me off a whole bunch of visits in a row. So many, in fact,
that my wife began to like having me home on Thursday nights. It
gave her an excuse not to have to play mah-jongg with her mother.
Finally though, I told Jennifer I absolutely had to see her.

One little preface. She was the only one I really loved. Honest.
My wife was never much more than a friend, sort of. And the others
I fooled around with . . . well, when you've got a roving eye, it
just looks for places to land out of habit. I realize that's not very
flattering to them—and I admit it's a hell of a lot less of a pitch
than the one I handed out, but . . .

On second thought, no buts. It's the truth. In the back of
my mind, I always had this kind of "saver" about Jennifer. I'd tell
myself I didn't really want to be messing around—that someday,
when push finally came to shove, I'd confess the whole story to her,
knock it off with all the others, and everything would be perfect.

It shows you how much I know about women. The first thing
Jennifer does when she gets her suspicions up about me is to start
seeing this Bruno, or whoever, again. And sleeping with him, too,
of course. This is to teach me a lesson, even though I don't know
anything about it. Ha!

Don't even listen to me. Smart remarks from stupid people, you
don't need. What actually happened was, when I finally get her to
agree to a Thursday visit again and we go to Jerry's restaurant for
dinner, she makes small talk through the whole meal till dessert
comes. Then she starts in with this offhand, "I'll be frank and you
be earnest" routine, and she unloads the whole thing on me: how
she figured I was probably cheating on her; and how before I got
a chance to do any more damage, she decided to beat me to it by
climbing into bed with Carlo, it turns out his name was. She then

spears a forkful of cheesecake, sits back as calmly as you please and
says, "How do you feel about that?"

It's lucky I have a big chin to start with, otherwise it'd be worn
away from leading with it. Brilliantly, I figure this is my opening. So,
partly because I really am a forgiving person—and partly because
I have this shrewd idea that if I set a good example, she'll have to
forgive me too—I tell her I want her more than anybody in the
world and that I think as long as two people love each other, they
can always find a way to forgive.

I reach over to take one of her hands, but she has them in her
lap. All she says is, "The only reason I met you tonight is that I've
decided to break it off."

I don't know what I expected, but it wasn't that. A little sweat
starts on my forehead. I ask her, "You don't love this Carlo, do
you?"

"No," she says, "but that's what I've decided. What about
you?"

Like a dummy, I start all over about how much I love her, but
she shakes that one off like the wrong pitch. "Frank and earnest,
remember? Your turn."

I guess I set myself up for it, but I honestly didn't think so at the
time. I told her everything. Even that there had been four others.
But it was over now, I said. I only wanted her; and even though I
knew it was rotten to have to dump on her like this, I was glad it
finally came out. It was actually a relief, because now I could really
change. And I would. Could she forgive me, too?

She said she needed time to think, so for some dumb reason, I
didn't press it. Instead, I called for the check and we left.

Unfortunately, we had two cars that night. (I had some business to do in the morning, so I'd picked up a rental at the airport).
When we got out to the parking lot, I gave her a kiss through the
window of her car and got into mine to follow her.

Maybe I was just an incurable optimist, or maybe I was only a
jerk about women, but I actually felt pretty good. Like, now there
could be a whole new start, and that I would actually consider ask-

ing Shirley for a divorce—God knows she'd mentioned it enough—
and that finally I'd be faithful to somebody for good.

The drive to her apartment took ten minutes and, when we got
there, I don't think it took me thirty seconds more than her to find
a parking place. Still, all of a sudden, I had a feeling something was
wrong, so I ran. I got into the lobby just in time to see her standing
by an open elevator at the far end. "Hey! Wait for me," I said in
what I thought was a fun voice. All she said was, "No, Marvin,"
and the door closed.

And that, believe it or not, was that. The end. Finished. Ka-
put. I went up to the apartment, of course, but she wouldn't let me
in. I guess I panicked. I couldn't get an elevator, so I ran five flights
down to the lobby and called her on the pay phone. She just said,
"Look, it's no use," and hung up. I tried three other phones on my
way to find a motel: two times, she just said the same thing; the
third time she talked, but she was like ice. Over and over, she kept
saying, "*Four*! How *could* you?"

When I finally got a room, I pulled myself together enough to
work out what I was going to say to her. I would begin with how
much I loved her, and how I really was making a new start; and then
I'd tell her I was never so sorry about anything in my life, but if I
didn't ask her, "How could *she*?" wouldn't she please do the same
for me? I even made a little ceremony out of unpacking and getting
ready for bed before I called. The wait killed me, but I figured I had
to give her time. I guess I thought it would be a kind of magic to
make everything right again. Whatever it was, by the time I dialed
her, I actually believed it was going to work. Such a dope! She
never even answered the phone.

I won't bore you with the rest. In the first place, there wasn't
any—at least not any I wanted. And in the second, you can probably write the ending yourself: all the phone calls followed by clicks
when she heard who it was; and, the few times she didn't hang up,
all the talk that got absolutely nowhere. You probably even know
which was worse. With no answer, at least you don't keep flogging
a dead hope.

I suppose everybody, at least when they're kids, believes deep down that if you get to the point of straightening out your act, the world is under some kind of obligation to stand up and cheer. But I must hold a record for lasting till I was forty-six without ever once catching on to the world's crummiest truth. Namely, that the day you finally do decide to dive in and swim for your life is always and exactly one day after somebody drained the pool.

But enough. As I said, except for Spencer's rallies and Jerry's talks, Cleveland had all the appeal of a morgue. I hardly even knew why I was going back there, but I did. Then one night, while I'm lying in bed feeling sorry for myself in a Holiday Inn, the phone rings.

The voice is somebody I never heard before. She has a kind of crackly, high-pitched, old-lady sound and a southern accent that's hard to place.

"Is this Mr. Marvin Goodman?"

I say yes, but before I can ask who it is, she tells me Jerry gave her my number. By now, I don't wonder about such things, so I just lie there and say, "What can I do for you?"

"Mr. Goodman, I'm Maybelle Caldwell—Spencer Caldwell's mother?" (The voice goes up at the end, Texas-style, but I don't say anything, so she keeps going.)

"If it's not too much of an imposition, I'd like to ask you to do a little favor for Barbara and me?"

Barbara, incidentally, turns out to be Barbara Horvath, Jerry's mother. But that's another story. Right now, I just say, "Sure, if I can. What is it?"

"As you may know, Jerry is planning to leave his restaurant work soon and devote himself full-time to the New Order."

I don't know this, so I say, "Oh. What exactly is he going to do?" She says she doesn't know much more herself, except that Jerry is definitely going to go through Spencer's ritual on the lake shore some Saturday soon and could I help her throw a little party for the two boys the night before? What it boils down to, of course, is that I'm supposed to spring for the bill. But since she wants to discuss the guest list, she asks me can I come to her house some time tomorrow?

If there's one thing I've learned in all this business with Jerry and Spencer—not to mention Jennifer—it's that since I always ended up saying yes, even to things I didn't want, I could save myself a lot of trouble by not saying no in the first place. Besides, I really was curious. Two psychic old ladies in one afternoon was more than I could resist. I say, "You have a deal, Mrs. Caldwell. How do I get to your place?"

She gives me what sound like pretty sketchy directions, so I start to ask her for a repeat. But she keeps right on babbling about how much she and Barbara appreciate this, and how they're looking forward to meeting me because the boys have told them so many nice things, and how . . . I forget what else; because while I'm waiting for an opening and reminding myself to ask her what time?, all of sudden she just clicks off.

I stare at the receiver for awhile and then, clear as a bell, the words "three o'clock" come into my head. "Aha!" I say out loud, "ESP, no less. This lady could put Ma Bell out of business." After that though, I hang up the dead phone, lean back on the pillow, and get the empty feeling in my stomach all over again.

Since Jennifer, I think you understand, this is not my favorite way of saying goodbye.

3

The directions to Maybelle Caldwell's place turned out to be even sketchier than I thought.

Actually, the only solid piece of information she gave me was the number of the freeway exit. After that, it was all "Turn left at the Mobil station" (she meant Exxon) and, "Go two blocks past the grocery on the right" (it should have been four and it was a deli). She did give me the address, 78 Aspen—"where the tree streets begin"—but since I never found even a Maple, it didn't help much.

The neighborhood was okay, but definitely not fancy. Two-story frame houses, mostly—built, I'd say, in the late twenties, but with a lot of turnover since. I drove around till I was totally lost and finally pulled over at an intersection with no signs at all. There was a black kid standing there, so I asked him Does he know where Aspen street is?

He just stares at me and grunts, "You here, man."

Since this is a nice surprise, I make a little joke. "Well, well. I finally found the trees, huh? I guess when you get to the woods, they figure you shouldn't expect signs."

"Hallowe'en, man."

It takes me a couple of seconds to work out that this is his idea of an explanation. "Oh, right," I say. "You wouldn't happen to know which way I turn to find number 78, would you?"

"No turn, man," he says, aiming his thumb at the side of the house I'm pulled up next to. "Thass it."

"Figures," I mumble as I start to parallel park.

"Huh?" he asks.

"Never mind," I tell him. "Thanks, anyway." He watches while I bump my way in and then walks off, giving me a look like he was Baryshnikov at a senior citizens dance. Kids!

The number on the house, incidentally, turns out to be a 7 followed by two nail holes. I ring the bell and put my sixth sense to work. Even if there isn't a sound after I try a house, I can always tell if somebody's home. I developed the knack when I was a kid delivering for a butcher. A place with people in it—even people fast asleep—gives off a different vibration. Other delivery boys used to come back with all kinds of stories about how nobody was there. Mr. Weintraub would just shake his head and say, "Go again, this time with Marvie. He's the only one I'll take his word."

I waited quite a while on Maybelle's steps, but I felt the right vibration, so I didn't even ring twice. Eventually she came.

"Mrs. Caldwell? I'm Marv . . ."

"Do come in, Mr. Goodman. My, my. You're the soul of punc-tuality, aren't you? The clock is just about to strike three."

I must say, some people I zero in on pretty good. Just from her telephone voice, I got her almost a hundred percent right. The white hair in a bun, the round face, the pink complexion, the shoes, with laces—even, I'm not kidding, the Westminster chimes on the clock. The only thing I was off on was her height. I guess Spencer threw me. I had her pegged as medium, but she was lucky if she broke five feet. All I can say is, Mr. Caldwell senior must have had *some* genes.

She takes my coat, puts it over the banister in the hall and shows me into the living room. The house is one of those front-to-back jobs, so when she sits me on the sofa, I find myself looking straight through the dining room into what I assume is the kitchen. Maybelle takes a chair across from me on the right, but to be honest with you, it took me a little while even to notice where she went.

Back in the kitchen, there is this girl in a black leotard doing yoga exercises. I know I already told you I have a roving eye, but don't let that throw you off. *Anybody* would have had a hard time not looking. First of all, not too many bodies are in that kind of shape—really together, I mean. So much so that I figure cynically that her face, if I ever got to see it, would have to be a letdown. But second, she was a real expert.

My wife Shirley does a little yoga now and then, so I know the names of some of the positions. When I sat down she was doing what they call the plow. Every time Shirley tries it, it looks unfortunately like a pile of laundry with hands and feet sticking out in funny places, but with this girl it was gorgeous—all straight lines and perfect curves. Also, a waist. My God! Twenty-two inches, tops.

Next she does the bow and, after that, one I never saw except in pictures. She sits in the lotus position, rocks back and forth a little, then sticks her hands down between her legs and lifts herself right off the floor, still holding the lotus. It's not exactly beautiful—even with her, it's a lot like a chicken—but it's absolutely incredible.

All this time, of course, I'm out to lunch as far as Maybelle Caldwell is concerned. Suddenly, I'm aware she's repeating my name so I turn toward her a little and shade my left eye with my had to cut off the view from the kitchen.

"As I was saying, Mr. Goodman, Barbara will be with us in a few minutes." I'm dying, of course, to ask who this girl in the kitchen is, but I force myself to remember why I'm here. "Oh, good," I say. "I've been looking forward to meeting Mrs. Horvath for a long time." Just to be extra friendly though, I ask her, "Meanwhile, why don't you just call me Marvin?"

My left hand slips a little and I see the girl go into a headstand. I don't know what that suggests to you, but let me tell you, you've never seen one like this. She sits on her heels, puts her elbows on the floor and then, without one false move, goes slower than anything you ever saw straight up toward the ceiling. It was like watching a tree grow right in front of your eyes.

Once, again, this is the kiss of death for my conversation with Maybelle Caldwell. Only after about a week do I hear her saying, "What I asked you, Marvin, was whether you had a middle name?"

"Oh, yes," I say. "It's Howard. Marvin Howard Goodman."

She reaches over to a table and picks up a pad and pencil. "Perhaps, while we wait, you'll let me do your numerology? Would you like that?"

"Sure," I say. "What do you need from me?"

"Only your name. It's quite painless, I assure you."

"That's good," I kid her a little. "Anything hurts more than an eye chart, I'm a terrible coward. Listen, though. I have an older brother. Maybe you could do the two of us for the price of one. He's got the same names."

"How do you mean?"

"My mother had a sense of humor, or something. She called him Howard Marvin and just switched the names around when she got to me. That would give us the same numerology, right?"

"Oh, no, Marvin. You still have two different *first* names. Just wait and see."

She sat there and scribbled on the pad for a minute, so I don't have to tell you where my eyes went. Still the headstand. Still straight. Still . . . still. Unbelievable.

Which is also the only thing I can say about Maybelle's numerology when she finally unloaded it on me. Let me give you just the highlights.

She tells me first some stuff Howie and I are supposed to have in common—love of pleasure and beauty, good management sense, ability to deal with dramatic changes. But then she starts in on the differences. I'm the adventurous one: impulsive, romantic, fascinated by the opposite sex, likely to have a lot of affairs. Howie is more balanced, with good judgment, lots of money, lots of kids—a terrific father and a loyal husband.

I give what I guess is a nervous laugh and she comes right back with a little extra. It's not that Howie couldn't be tempted to stray. In fact, it's almost a certainty that he would. But only once, and it would be something he'd handle without hurting a soul.

I tell you this because, while a lot of the other things could apply to almost anybody, that last one really hit it on the head about Howie. He did have an affair once nine years ago, and it worked out exactly the way she said. The amazing thing was that I was the only one he ever told and I never breathed a word about it. Not even to Jerry. Maybelle Caldwell made me feel as if she was looking right through the top of my head.

We talked a while longer. The girl in the kitchen disappeared— which was just as well, because Maybelle switched subjects so fast I needed all the concentration I could manage. Finally though, she stops dead, listens to some sound I can't hear, and announces, "Good. That will be Barbara now."

Like a gentleman, I get up and take a couple of steps toward the staircase I presume she's coming down. Like a dummy, I don't even turn around when Maybelle says, "Barbara, this is Marvin Howard Goodman. Marvin, this is Barbara Horvath, Jerry's mother."

Eventually, of course, it dawns on me that the lady is already in the room, so I do a one-eighty. My mouth, I think, falls open, but nothing comes out. Instead, my brain goes into overload.

First of all, as you can guess, she's the girl from the kitchen— except that now she's put on a pair of paint-smeared jeans and she has a blue silk scarf tied around her neck. Second, she's carrying three glasses of wine balanced on a notebook. Third, while she's obviously not the twenty-year old I thought I saw two rooms away, she looks not a day over thirty-five. Fourth, since Jerry's now thirty himself, I know she has to be pushing fifty, rock bottom, so I look for gray hair. There isn't any.

In my line of work I see a lot of women. One thing I can spot a mile off is a dye job. Not here though. This is brown hair with about two hundred highlights to the square inch, plus the kind of natural wave most women would kill for. And cut just right, besides: not too young, and therefore not old at all.

Fifth and last though, my conclusion about her face goes straight out the window. The body, of course, is very definitely still there—once again, everything just right, nothing too much—but the face . . . Honestly, I'm just gonna give up on a description. It made you fall in love right on the spot.

I think I got something like "How do you do" out of my mouth, but I don't remember it. All I know is that when I eventually took the wine she was handing me, I sat down and couldn't think of a thing to say. Which, as you know, has got to be a first.

She sees this and starts a little nothing conversation with May-belle about dinner until my brain comes back from lunch. Then she says, in this nice kind of dusky voice, "I see you survived Maybelle's directions. When I listen to them, I have visions of people orbiting Euclid forever. Like Charlie on the MTA."

The accent is a little bit New York, but with the r's put in and the snarl left out. She also smiles, which helps my tongue come unstuck.

"Well, Mrs. Horvath . . ." I have no idea why I call her that, because it sounds just wrong, but all she says is "Barbara—please." So I start again.

"Well, Barbara . . ." This sounds even wronger but what else is there? "I got good and lost, until one of your friendly neighborhood guides set me straight—after, of course, I was already here."

"Of course," she smiles. "The guide, by the way, was probably Timmy—unless he talked a blue streak, in which case, it was his brother Greg. They live around the corner and insist on keeping an eye on us. In any case, they're invited to the dinner too."

"This one was definitely not the blue streaker. Look, though. While we're on the subject of the party, let me tell you what I had in mind. I figured maybe Jerry would like to eat Chinese for a change, so I took the liberty of reserving a private room at my fa-vorite place. That okay? If I tell them to leave out the MSG, maybe even Spencer will break down and have a vegetable something."

I get this last remark out before I remember Maybelle is also in the room, so I try to cover it with something dumb about how my favorite dish is Buddhist Delight. Maybelle, however is busy with the numerology pad again and Barbara just smiles. "Oh, Spencer," she says quietly and then, so quick I almost miss it, she rolls her eyes and with two fingers imitates running straight up the wall.

"No need to spare me," Maybelle says without looking up. "He'd drive anybody crazy—even if he is my son. All that brown rice is turning his complexion the color of library paste."

I swallow a laugh and go back to setting up the party. The Chi-nese restaurant gets the okay, but not the Friday after next which was when I made the reservation for. Maybelle remembers Jerry has to be at a wedding reception on, as she puts it, "the second Saturday after next." So, since Jerry wants the dinner the night before he gets his shirt and stone from Spencer, she says that means there's only one possible Saturday for Spencer's ceremony and therefore only next Friday for the party.

This confuses me. As far as I'm concerned, there's another Friday and Saturday in there somewhere. I explain that next Friday, unfortunately, is not so hot for me, so could we maybe make it the one after that? This, of course, confuses Maybelle, since to her that's the Friday she already said was no good.

Finally, Barbara remembers about New Yorkers and how they count days. She translates for me.

"What Maybelle means is that the Saturday *after* next is out. *Next* Saturday is Jerry's day with Spencer, so next Friday has to be the dinner. Got it?"

"That's ridiculous," Maybelle butts in. "Next Saturday is *tomorrow*."

"Not in New York it isn't," I tell her. "That's *this* Saturday. Don't worry though. We're all saying the same thing."

"But not in English," she says, standing up. "I'm going to start supper. Call me when there's something I can understand."

"She's not sore, is she?" I ask Barbara after she bustles out of the room.

"No. Just eighty-one."

This is a lead I absolutely cannot resist. I know we haven't done the guest list yet, but since maybe I'll never get the chance again, I jump right on it.

"That reminds me," I say in the most offhand voice I can manage. "I don't know why, but I sort of figured you and she would be around the same age. As it turns out, she's a lot older than I thought, and you're . . . well . . . I don't know . . . I never . . ."

I suppose I would have rattled on like that forever, but she finally put me out of my misery with a big smile: "I'm forty-six, Marvin. I had Jerry when I was sixteen."

That makes her, of course, exactly my age, and since I haven't got my nerve back to ask her anything direct yet, I say, "Hey! A coincidence. I was born in 1935, too. When's your birthday?"

"September eighth."

I remember Spencer's remark about astrology, so I figure I'll impress her a little while I'm dawdling. "Mine's September twentieth. That makes us both Virgos, right?"

"No, Marvin," she says. "At least not in the system I use. You're a Virgo, I'm a Leo."

"Oh," I say, waiting for her to go on. She doesn't though. "Maybelle and I are really not all that much of a mystery. She was the first child of the oldest of five sisters and I was the last child of the youngest. Simple?"

"Ah!" I agree. "So much for the thirty-five-year spread."

"If you like puzzles, though," she smiles, "I've got three children older than I am. Fifty-three, fifty-one and forty-eight, to be exact."

She gives me a minute to figure this one. "Step-children?" I finally ask.

"Yes. Plus two more, younger. And Jerry, of course. I married a widower."

Once again, I start doing numbers in my head. I try to get a fix on the age of Mr. Whoever Horvath when he married her, but all I come up with is a picture of the thousand-year-old man and a teenager. Barbara, however, is obviously playing me for what it's worth, so I just go along: "How old was *he* when you got married?"

"Forty-nine. After Stefan's wife died, I used to sit the younger ones for him. He was an electrician in a hospital during the day, but he also did house jobs on his own time at night."

It's amazing how the human brain can go from not being able to do even rough arithmetic on somebody's age to cooking up a full-dress scandal "Aha!" I think to myself. "The old baby-sitter routine. Wiring wasn't all he did at night." Right away, though, I feel funny, so I make a feeble remark about how he was a lucky man to find *her*.

"No, Marvin," she says to me. "*I* was the lucky one. He was the best man in the world. Really. That's the only way to say it. And he was as good to Jerry as he was to his own children."

She drops this one on me with a perfectly straight face. Obviously, the only conclusion I can draw is that she must've been pregnant by somebody else when Horvath married her, but this makes me feel twice as funny, so I just refuse to draw it.

I know. You're going to tell me things like that happen all the time, so where do I, of all people, get off being so fussy? Especially since it was apparently a more terrific marriage than anything I ever ran into. Well. The answer is, I don't know. It's just what I found myself thinking.

Anyway, I do a quick scramble—which she does me the favor of not noticing—and come up with one of the famous M. H. Goodman conversational saves: "He died, huh? When?"

I don't know if you study smiles the way I do, but if you ever did, you've got to know that only one person in a million can smile at you after a remark like that and not look like some kid pulling the wings off a fly. I mean, anything but a straight face is going to make you feel like a jerk. What can I tell you though? She brought it off as if it was nothing.

"He died fifteen years ago, Marvin. At sixty-one. He'd had a string of coronaries—so many that he used to kid about them. He told me to make sure and sell his heart after he died, but not to a Hungarian. He said God made enough bad jokes on them already. You'd have liked him. You have the same sense of humor."

At this point, of course, I have two sensations. One is that I'm ten feet tall. The other unfortunately, is that my knees have turned to mayonnaise. Mr. Smoothie, who never fails to respond even to total indifference, gets the welcome of his dreams and can't make a move. Instead, out comes the second Goodman save: "You never remarried?"

She just laughs and asks if I know the definition of a Hungarian. I'm about to say yes, but she starts it anyway: "A Hungarian is a man who can get into a revolving door behind you . . ."

". . . and come out ahead of you," I finish in chorus with her.

"It's the story of my life, I guess." And we both smile. And that's that. The biggest, shortest romance on record.

Naturally, my tongue is the first thing to recuperate. "What'd you do though? I mean, Jerry had to be like, fifteen when your husband died. Did you go to work?"

"No. Between Stefan's pension and what he made off the books, I didn't have to. I had this house free and clear so I took in Maybelle and went back to school. High school first, then college, then graduate school."

"How far did you get?—and what in, if I'm not being nosy."

"Political science," she says. "All I've got left is the orals on my doctoral dissertation."

I should have known I was out of my depth. "What's it about?"

"Vico," she says.

On this I draw a complete blank. I wouldn't know Vico, a pizza maker, from VeeCo, a rocket-fin manufacturer. "Hmmm," I say.

"An Italian philosopher—seventeenth/eighteenth century," she explains. "He was very in when I started. Now, you couldn't trade five Vicos for a Pete Rose."

"Hey! You a baseball fan, too?"

"Of course," she laughs.

"What else?" I say.

"Lots."

"Like?"

"Everything except cooking."

"That's funny. Knowing Jerry, I mean. Where do you suppose he got . . ." Once again, my foot goes straight in and plugs up my mouth.

"Marvin," she says, "Relax. I've been his mother for thirty years, so stop worrying about saying the right thing. Besides. He's a Cancer. They're born food pushers."

"Okay," I say. "What's you number-one best thing?"

"Painting. What's yours?"

"Being a klutz. If I gotta have a specialty, it's not going to be something I run second in. Seriously, though. Would you mind if I asked you a question about Jerry?"

"No." She says this without any hesitation, but I pick up a change in her. Not much. Maybe she just shifted in her chair. Whatever it was, I suddenly find myself playing down what I had in mind.

"When I first met him, he was onto this idea about dying and rising. He hasn't mentioned it since—at least not to me—but I was wondering if he ever talked about it to you." I deliberately leave out the part about his saying he was God.

She gives a little wave with her hand. "Sometimes," she says. "There isn't much we haven't discussed. Why?"

"Well, according to Spencer, he has these powers—to do miracles, I mean. But do you think he could actually come back from the dead?"

"Yes," she answers, and just drops the subject.

"Oh," I say.

"Don't worry, Marvin. I have problems with it too."

"Thanks," I tell her. "That makes me feel better. Misery loves company, I guess. He must've been a handful to raise, huh?"

The big smile comes back. "He certainly wasn't easy. It's funny, though. People act as if their kids' badness would be the biggest problem. Actually, it's goodness that hardly anyone can handle. It always comes twelve sizes too large."

"I never thought of it that way."

"Almost nobody does. But then, not many families are as peculiar as ours."

"What do you mean? With the powers and all? Don't tell me you have them, too?"

This is a little nervy of me, but she doesn't seem to mind. As simple as you please, she tells me, yes, she has them; it's just that she never tries to use them.

"Spencer once did a telephone thing with my watch. It was amazing."

"I heard," she says as if she thought it was a waste of time. "I guess that's just not my style."

At first, I figure this means I'm supposed to drop the subject; actually, she's just mulling it over in her mind. "The powers I have aren't really miraculous. At least I don't think they are."

"What kind are they then?"

"Well, for one thing, I can sometimes see the future—if I look. Mostly, though, I just refuse to."

"How come? A lot of people would give their eye teeth to know what's coming at them."

"I know, but that's silly. When the future gets here, it'll be just another *now* they have to deal with. Until it does, they're better off working on the *now* they've got."

"You don't tell fortunes, then? What about astrology?"

"I hate it when it's used that way. Fatalism doesn't need any more encouragement than it already has."

"I guess you're right," I say. "But you mentioned *powers*. You have others too?"

"Only one. Ever since I was a child, I've known I can die when I want to—actually will my own death, that is."

"You mean, without taking anything, or . . ."

"Yes. Just by commanding my heart to stop."

"Why would you want to do a thing like that?"

"I'm not sure. In any case, there obviously hasn't been a reason to yet."

"That's good."

"I think so. But it is what it is. When the time comes . . ."

"What were you going to say?"

"Oh, only that the subject is pointless. When I finally do it, it'll be something nobody—I, especially—can prove a thing about anyway. Better not to dwell on it at all."

"That I'll buy. But listen. I should really be going, so maybe we could finish up about the dinner. I need a number."

"Let's see," she says, ticking off the names on her fingers.

"There's Maybelle and myself. Then you—and your brother Howard, if he can make it. Jerry made a special point of that."

"Howie hasn't even met Jerry."

She shrugged. "He will if he comes. Then there's my Aunt Ruth, and there's Dieter Schmidt, Carol Peterson and Beth Murphy—Jerry knows them from cooking school—and there's also a Jennifer Ranieri I've only heard about. I think she's the one Jerry helped out when she was in trouble with the Syndicate, but I may be wrong."

This is a total surprise. Talk about mixed emotions . . .

"And finally, there are the two Waters boys and Curtis Brock. That's twelve, plus Jerry of course."

"Right," I say. "Most of them I've heard of, but who are those last three?"

"Oh. Timmy and Greg Waters are the two black boys from around the corner. You ran into Timmy outside, remember? His brother Greg, the champion talker, conned us into inviting them both. I'm afraid we don't run the world's tightest ship around here."

"It's better that way, believe me. Who's Curtis Brock?"

"Curtis is a lawyer. Very bright. Very capable. Very black. And very gay."

There are some remarks you only take in after you've had the chance to play them back in your head. This one went by me so fast the first time, all I noticed was that it seemed a little clipped for her. That it was totally out of character, I didn't figure out till I woke up in the night hearing those four 'verys' pounding in my head. But *why* it was out of character is something which, unfortunately, I didn't find out till much, much later. Too late, really . . . but that's a different part of the story.

At the moment, I just ignored it, made some small talk and finished my wine. "By the way," I said, "What's the dinner actually for? I mean, I know it's just before Jerry and Spencer do their thing, but is there something else maybe? This Chinese restaurant is terrific when it comes to parties with themes. They make dragons out of cold hors d'oeuvres,—peacocks, any animal you could think of, in fact. With a little hint, they could do something spectacular."

"I don't think that'll be necessary, Marvin. Jerry does have something in mind, but it's not for me to say. You'll see."

"Listen, it's okay," I tell her as I get up for my coat. "I like a little mystery myself."

She walks me to the door and, just before I start down the steps, she says, "Oh. Marvin. There is one thing you could ask the restaurant to do. Just for me."

"Sure," I say. "All you have to do is name it."

"Absolutely no fortune cookies," she says, and shuts the door.

4

I was back and forth to Cleveland as usual the next two weeks, but between the dinner and the ceremony and the wedding reception, things were hectic. I know it doesn't sound like it, but I was even squeezing in a little business now and then. In fact, the only time I got a few minutes to think was on the return flight to New York the night of the reception.

I actually went as far as scribbling some notes on an envelope, but unfortunately my sense of organization gave out after that and I left them on the plane. It doesn't matter, though, because I had them practically memorized. The reason was Shirley. I wanted to make sure I didn't leave out anything when I got home and dropped the bomb on her, namely, that I'd be spending all my time in Cleveland for awhile. That gets me ahead of the story, though, so let me go back and do the dinner first.

It was the first time I'd ever seen Jerry in a group. It hadn't dawned on me till then, but most of my conversations with him had been strictly one on one. He surprised me. I mean, I always knew he was convivial, but I never expected him to have so many different styles. One for everybody he talked to, practically.

For instance, when I introduced him to my brother, he didn't use any of that smartmouth horseplay he worked on me the first time I met him. It was as if he had an instinct for exactly what would go down with whoever. Howie, as I said, does a lot of kidding himself, but he expects other people basically just to feed him straight lines. Jerry played him perfectly. Instead of coming on strong, he sold himself short and left it up to Howie to make the pitch. In fact, he actually got him to deliver one of what I call his Monty Confucius lines. Jerry says to him, "Howie, after what Marvin must've told you, you deserve a lot of credit for even showing up here. Most people would have figured I was just a horse's ass and stayed home." Quick as a flash, Howie says to him, "Ah, so. You forget old Chinese proverb: When God speak truth through horse, wise man not make fuss about which end it comes out of."

On the other hand, with the two Waters kids he came across like a teenager: lots of kidding around and, at least twice in the evening, this kind of basketball team handslap where they'd all yell, "Yo!" and scatter. The younger one, Greg, obviously had something like a crush on him—following him around, sitting next to him—but it all seemed perfectly normal.

With Curtis Brock though, Jerry was Mr. Earnestness in person. They spent fifteen minutes together right at the beginning, looking like about as much fun as the board of Morgan Guaranty; but then Jerry started milling around and Curtis drifted over to me. I ended up sitting next to him at dinner.

I'm pretty sure I would have picked up on his preferences all by myself but Barbara's little eight-word summary didn't hurt. It was right on target in fact—provided, of course, you don't automatically assume gay and swishy are the same thing. If you've been in the garment business long enough, you get so you can spot even the butch types. Curtis was forty-two, tall—six-one, at least—and he had a fair amount of flesh on him. Very evenly distributed, though. Just a shade too evenly. With somebody his age, you expect a little pot; by then, if a guy likes women, he's learned that his waist is about the last thing that turns them on. But if he likes guys, nine times out of ten he'll have a figure, even he has to squeeze himself into it. *Sleek* I guess is the word I want for Curtis. Also, wound up tight in more places than the middle.

He and I spent most of the dinner talking about some affirmative action suit he was involved in. At least, he talked and I listened. Two things stuck out. For one, he really was smart. A genuine lawyer's mind. Tick, tick, tick; therefore, tick, tick: whammo! Somebody you'd feel very good not having him to do a number on you in front of a jury. Second, though, he was obviously turned on to Jerry.

What gave that away was how he kept an eye on him when Greg Waters was around. I may not be a psychiatrist, but I know jealousy when I see it. Not that he said anything. It was just that for all his brains, Curtis had a romantic itch he didn't know how to keep from scratching.

At the time, though, I just refused to add any of it up. That was partly because I really do try to keep an open mind about such things, but partly also because I was positive that as far as Jerry was concerned all the traffic on Curtis Street was strictly one way. All you had to do was see Jerry with the girls who were there.

He was nice to everybody, of course, but it was obvious he wasn't immune to the opposite sex. Especially if you picked up on the little differences in the way he used his eyes. With Beth Murphy, for instance—she was not only sort of plain, but also looked as if she had eaten her way through ten cooking schools—he had what I'd call his ordinary, bright look. You know. Attention, interest, playfulness. But nothing much else.

With Carol Peterson, though, who knew exactly when to stop filling a pair of jeans—or with Jennifer, I might add—his eyes did something I never never saw them do before: they just plain flirted. Maybe he wasn't aware of the signals he gave off any more than Curtis was, but they were there.

I know you'd probably like me to go on about this, but if it's all the same, I don't think I will. I may watch a lot, but I still try to give everybody as much space as I can. I figure, it's their lives. Curtis and Jerry, Jerry and pretty girls—I have enough trouble running Marvin's operation without trying to save other people from themselves. Especially since, of all the projects a human being could undertake, that's probably the number one loser of all time.

So I'll just finish up about the dinner with two things. Obviously, I had to talk to Jennifer—she even gave me a kiss and a big smile. But as far as the conversation was concerned, all I remember was that it kept spelling o-v-e-r in the back of my head. That was mostly my fault, I suppose, but what could I do? Marvin, unfortunately, is the one character who doesn't get enough distance from Marvin.

The other thing was the purpose of the dinner. Nobody even mentioned the subject till the end, but then Jerry gets up and makes this flat announcement that right after the ceremony tomorrow, he plans to appoint us all as witnesses. What we're supposed to do, he says, is give him a year or so—to "hang out" with him was what he actually said, but it was obvious he had something perfectly serious in mind. Anybody who wanted to sleep on it could take till tomorrow to say no; but he hoped we'd all say yes. And that was it, except for one thing that knocked me right off my chair.

Just before he finishes, he throws in, as if he'd thought it up right on the spot, "Oh. And Marvin will be the Chief Witness—if he's willing, of course." And then he sits down. I was going to say nobody was more surprised that I was, but that's not true. Curtis Brock looked like his brain had gone home and left his face behind. Everybody else seemed to think it was a terrific idea though, so before I had a chance to think, I heard myself say, "Sure. Why not?" Some things about me might have changed in the past two years, but getting in over my head in a hurry was not one of them.

Oh. There was one other thing about the dinner. Spencer wasn't there. At first I thought it was because he was afraid the white rice or something would upset his *Wa*, but then it dawned on me that Barbara hadn't even put him on the guest list. Which was funny, now that I thought of it. I mean, who'd be more of a natural witness than Spencer? All I came up with, though, was a feeling that maybe it had to do with her seeing into the future. Like, she just knew he wouldn't make the party. Or that maybe he wouldn't be around when the time came for witnessing. I also, of course, got a little creepy feeling about this family I was involved with. But you know me. Second thoughts are not my problem. I already make myself enough trouble with first ones.

Anyway, the dinner basically went off fine, now that I look back on it. In fact, it sort of sticks out in my mind as the last normal thing that happened to me. After that, it was one weird thing on top of another.

Which brings me, I guess, to the ceremony with Spencer the following Saturday. The day started out pretty good, if you like red sunrises, but by the time Spencer got rolling at noon, it had turned into one of those raw April jobs where it spits off and on but never actually rains. Anyway, we were stuck with it. Apparently, somebody had decided that Jerry would come up last, so we just hung around in the crowd till almost two: a good hour's worth of Spencer on how everything was coming apart at the seams, plus I don't know how many assorted types swearing off maybe a hundred different things.

Don't get the impression, though, that it was a set performance. Spencer may have had his list of pet poisons, but he left people free to renounce whatever they felt like. There were a lot of duplications, naturally. Coffee and chocolate took a drubbing from almost everybody—plus booze, of course. But I was surprised at how many—especially the young ones—also took a swipe at drugs.

After that, though, it was a free-for-all. Practically the only things that didn't get renounced were dirt, turnip greens and tofu. The list I made on the plane had a lot more on it, but here's a sample off the top of my head.

Not only meat, but vegetarian dishes that tried to look like meat. Colored toilet paper (because of dye). White toilet paper (because of sulfite). Name brands (because of the system). Store brands (because they're made by name brands). No-name brands (because they're still part of the system). Coal heat (mineral plunder). Oil heat (atmospheric blight). Wood heat from cutting live trees (vegetable murder). Wood heat from cutting dead trees (interfering with natural decay). Solar heat (it won't be feasible till the energy monopolies allow it; when they do, it'll be a con job along with everything else). Electricity, plastics, paper products, flush toilets, cesspools, sewage disposal plants, nuclear energy, income taxes, voting in elections, and working for a living.

It was the kind of performance which, if you listened to it straight through, made you feel guilty, virtuous, bored, fascinated, and in the end, just exhausted. Jerry's criticisms of it were actually too kind. He said he didn't agree with the *program* of Spencer's movement. The real trouble was that it had a thousand programs, not one of which was acceptable to more than six people. Maybe that's what he meant, though. The world is going to hell not just because the bad guys have a bad program, but even more because the good guys can't get together on any program at all. And they never will, I suppose he was saying. You watch goodness flounder around long enough, it only makes you sad.

But that's neither here nor there, I guess. Finally, when everybody who wanted a white shirt, a new name and a chance to spout off had had a turn, Jerry turns to us—all the witnesses except my brother Howie were there—and he says, "C'mon. We may as well get this over with." So up we go and we all stand in front of Spencer.

Let me tell you the rest as straight as possible. First of all, Spencer suddenly stops looking like Spencer. Obviously, somebody six-foot-seven can't actually shrink away to nothing, but that's exactly what seemed to happen. He just stopped presiding like he always did up there and looked like some kid waiting for directions. Not a word came out of his mouth. Finally, after about a minute goes by, Jerry leans over to him and says, "Hey, Spence. The sweatshirt, huh?"

"Oh," Spencer says. "Here." Instead of helping Jerry into it the way he usually did, he just leaves him to put it on himself. This is already pretty odd as far as I'm concerned, but compared to what came next, it's nothing.

Jerry gets the shirt on, flips up the hood the way they were all supposed to, and then pulls the zipper all the way up to the neck— at which point, I'm not kidding, right out of nowhere comes this huge clap of thunder. I damn near jumped out of my skin. I mean, I know it was overcast and all, but it wasn't that kind of day. I couldn't have been more surprised if there hadn't been a cloud in the sky.

Jerry, though, hardly seemed to pay any attention to it—except that when he heard the crowd's reaction, he got a black look on his face. What happened was that for a second or two after the thunder there was absolute silence. Then, all of a sudden, this stoned-looking kid in the front row starts yelling "God spoke to him" and all hell breaks loose. Half the crowd begins repeating what the kid is saying while the other half keeps telling each other it was only thunder. Typical.

Obviously, at least as far as I'm concerned, it had to be some kind of sign. But people are hopeless when it comes to such things. They're like a dog: you point to something and what does he do? He smells your finger. Give a crowd a sign and in ten seconds the only thing they'll be doing is arguing about the lettering.

Oh, well. As I said, Jerry was a lot angrier about it than I was, but he controlled himself. All he said was, "C'mon, Spence. Let's keep going. The stone."

Spencer was still half in a fog but he came out of it enough to start mumbling something about how Jerry should be the one giving the stone to him and not vice versa, and how, till now, he never really understood—whatever that meant. I think he would have knelt down on the spot, except that Jerry grabbed him and kept him up.

The crowd was still in an uproar so I missed a lot of what they said to each other. Spencer's voice was too low to hear, and Jerry just kept repeating himself: "It's okay, Spence. It's okay. Just give me the stone. It's all right, no matter who does it." Things like that—all ending with Spencer refusing to write a name on the stone for Jerry, and Jerry taking it and saying once more, "Don't worry, Spence. Everything's okay."

By this time, the black look is off Jerry's face and he just seems drained. So I say to him, "Speaking of which, you don't look all that okay to me. You want to get away from here? My car is pretty close."

"Don't worry, Marvin," he says. "I'll manage. Just get the rest of the witnesses around me and start walking into the crowd. Oh. And tell them they're appointed, huh? I almost forgot that. Also, you might mention I won't be around much this week. I'll see you all at the wedding next Saturday."

I want, of course, to ask him where he's going and why, but I figure there'll be time after we get through, so I herd the eleven of us around him and get them moving. I suppose we looked like a flying wedge because at first the crowd starts to let us through. But once they realize it's Jerry, they close up like a vise and stop us dead. For a minute there, I'm a little scared, but then suddenly Curtis Brock puts all his 210 pounds behind his shoulder, roars "Back off!" at the top of his voice, and through we go.

"Hey! Terrific," I say to him as we come out in the open. "With an offensive line like that, we should try for the Super Bowl before we straighten up the world." Then I turn around and start to say something to Jerry about yardage and rushing, but I get only as far as "Hey! Jer . . ."

"Where'd he go" I ask Curtis. "He's not back in that crowd is he? There's no telling what they might . . ."

"Jerry's fine," Curtis says with a smile. "He just went, that's all. He does it every now and then."

"But how . . . ?"

"I don't know, Marvin. If you ever get so you can *see* a disappearance, maybe you can explain it to me."

5

Before I go any further, I have to fill you in about my home life, such as it was.

Over the past two years I hadn't exactly told Shirley a whole lot about Jerry. I mentioned, of course, that I'd met him, and that between the restaurant and here and there, I'd seen quite a bit of him. But I never said a word about what I was getting involved with.

That was partly because at the beginning I wasn't so sure of it myself, and partly because even after I was, it still embarrassed me to talk about it. But also, with Shirley already suspicious about me and other women, I figured if I told her only ordinary things about my trips to Cleveland, she'd be less likely to pick up on my love life. So, back when I was still seeing Jennifer, I just fed Shirley details about what a terrific cook Jerry was and how he made his different specialties. Even before the affair broke up though, the smokescreen blew back in my face.

Shirley's mother Rhoda, who lives with us, has two topics of conversation. When she's got something ailing her—which is 75 percent of the time—she talks about what's wrong with Rhoda. When she's healthy, the subject is what's wrong with me. Unfortunately, one of my spiels about Jerry must've coincided with a night she felt pretty good, because all she had to hear was "young guy" and she jumped straight to the conclusion I was a bisexual who was finally going gay.

"Look at him" she says. "A year ago, he was getting gray like anybody his age should. Now what's happening? Grecian Formula,

I'll bet. That's what they all use, you know. They can't stand it when they don't look like Adonises any more."

Shirley, of course, uses this to unload one of her little zingers on me. "Oh, I don't think so Momma. Whatever Marvin's got cooking in Cleveland, it's definitely not some guy in front of a restaurant stove."

"You mean it's a girl chef?" Rhoda comes right back, not noticing the subject is getting away from her. "What could she see in him? Mr. Gourmet! Ha! He can't even make tea with a bag."

Enough of that, though. Let's just say that between my involvements, Shirley's jealousy, and Rhoda's mouth, apartment 7G, 170 West End Avenue was not my idea of a nice place to come home to. Still, there I was in the elevator at 9:45 on the night of the wedding reception, hoping mostly they would have gone to bed.

They hadn't. No sooner am I in the door but Rhoda starts groaning from the couch and Shirley puts her finger in her free ear so I shouldn't talk to her while she's on the phone. As welcomes go, this is about a five on a scale of ten for my house, so I just put down my suitcase and open the bakery box Jerry gave me before I left.

Remember I told you he said he'd be out of circulation for a week after the thing with Spencer? Well, he was. When he finally showed up the following Friday night, he said he'd been on a retreat; but as far as I could see, he spent it in a bakery. He'd made all kinds of fancy stuff for the reception: mocha cakes, plum tarts, chestnut boats, you name it. Also, something I don't know the right name for but I call zebra cake, with chocolate icing and white stripes and apricot glaze underneath—fantastic. And napoleons and eclairs and petit fours in baskets made out of ribbon candy and about nine different kinds of cookies, every one better than the last. Anyway, there was so much, that even a reception twice the size wouldn't have finished it all, so when we left, everybody got a doggie box. Mine had strawberry tarts and the thin wafers with pieces of almond that are my favorite.

I sit down with the box, and while Rhoda groans and Shirley keeps chewing somebody's ear off, I help myself to two tarts and a

fistful of cookies. Rhoda, I gather from Shirley's phone conversation, is having another one of her diverticulitis attacks. The only
doctor she'll let treat her is out of town till Monday morning, so I
figure I'm in for my least favorite kind of weekend.

I know my mother-in-law is sick and all, and normally I'm a
very sympathetic person. But one thing I simply cannot stand is
the way she becomes a monomaniac on the subject of her bowels
when she has these attacks. The minute Shirley hangs up, Rhoda
starts in.

"Tell him I'm sick and can't talk," she says. "While you were
on the phone, I had another movement. I think there's a little less
blood in the stool, but I can't be sure. At least it's not diarrhea and
fresh bleeding."

"What did she eat this time?" I whisper, hoping that Rhoda
won't hear.

"Cabbage and apple salad," Shirley says. "It's getting so that if
I leave her when she's the least bit hungry, she makes herself some
snack that practically tears her apart. I don't know what I'm going
to do."

At this point, Rhoda lets out an "Oh, my God!" and runs for
the bathroom. Shirley flops in a chair and says, "You go see if she's
all right. I've had all I can take." I wait a minute and then go knock
on the door and ask how she feels.

"Go away," she says. "It isn't too loose, but it's not as well-
formed as it should be. Tell Shirley I have to have my testing kit."

"Hey, Shirl," I yell, "where's her testing kit? Is that something
new? She says she wants it."

"It's new," Shirley says coming down the hall with this paper
folder. "It's got two little white squares inside. She puts a smear
from the beginning of the movement on one and from the end of
the movement on the other. If they turn blue, there are blood cells.
Obviously, when she can *see* the blood, she doesn't need it; but it
makes her feel better to use it, so I just humor her."

Since this practically makes me gag right on the spot, I go back
to the living room and wait. I should learn. Whenever I plan an
important conversation with somebody, I work it all out six differ-

ent ways so I'll be ready for anything. What happens, of course, is that some seventh thing I never thought of comes along and blows my plans to bits. In this case, the diverticulitis has obviously got Shirley in no mood for what I have to say about Jerry. In fact, I almost decide to put if off till the morning, but then Shirley comes out and says, "Well, you finally decided Cleveland could do without you for a couple of days, huh?"

I used to be a person who tried to break things gently, but in the last couple of years, I'm not so fussy. Since people always seem to figure where my long, slow curves are going before I get even halfway through the windup, I figure I might as well just pitch them something they can hit right off. I say to Shirley, "Funny you should put it that way. As a matter of fact, I'm going to be staying in Cleveland full-time for about a year. That's the bad news. The rest, if you're interested, is all better."

She just sits here and shakes her head. "What's better? You've got two girlfriends this time instead of one?"

"C'mon, Shirl," I say to her. "I already told you. The last year and a half, there hasn't been anybody. I'm going to Cleveland for Jerry. He asked me to give him a year and I said yes."

"A year for what? Italian cooking?"

"No. For being a witness to certain things he's going to do. As a matter of fact, he's not even cooking anymore. He's kind of . . . preaching."

"Don't tell me you've got yourself mixed up in some cult! What am I supposed to do while you're out there getting religion? Starve to death?"

"Slow down," I tell her. "In the first place it's not really a religion—not if I understand Jerry right, that is. And in the second, I've got the money part of it all figured out. Irving's going to buy out my interest for half a million. I keep a hundred thousand for myself for however many years I can get out of it, the other four hundred thousand is yours. It should hold you till your mother dies, at which point your only worries will be nuclear."

"You know something?" she snaps at me. "You have absolutely

no taste. That poor woman is suffering in there and you have the gall to talk about her as if she were a bond about to mature."

Normally, this kind of approach backs me right off, but since the fat is already in the fire, I figure what the hell. "Listen, Shirley," I say. "Let's not get into taste. Your mother could use a little herself. All I said was that when she dies, she'll leave you a bundle. Why is it bad taste to mention things that happen to be true?"

"Humph!" she snorts. From Shirley, this is a lot, since it's as far as she ever goes admitting anybody else has a point. "This Jerry, though," she says, shifting gears. "What's so special about him?"

Once again, I decide straight out is best: "I think he just may actually be God. I know that's got to sound wild, but even so, I've decided to trust that he is."

"What does he do, glow in the dark?"

"No. It's not like that at all. He's actually very ordinary. A regular average person."

"Except he claims he's God. If you ask me, he's a regular average cuckoo."

"I know, I know," I tell her. "I went through all of that myself. It's just that when you know him, it's different. He makes sense."

"Makes sense? God shows up in the world, and he turns out to be a cook? What's he going to do, save the world with fettucine?"

"Shirley," I say, "if it's any comfort to you, my own first reaction to him was just about the same. Look. I know it sounds a little nervy, but I've really made up my mind. I have to do this."

"Nervy!" she shouts. "It sounds stupid, that's what. He just says he's God, and you believe him? No evidence, no proof?"

"For such a thing," I tell her, "how can there be proof? And as far as evidence is concerned, even if people actually *see* a miracle, they can still read it any way they like. The only two things you personally need to know is that my mind is made up and that you're taken care of."

"Oh, boy!" she says. "Mr. Toughie comes to town. I don't get any explanation at all? Not even a couple of so-called miracles to think about while you're gone?"

"I only saw him do one. This afternoon, in fact, at a wedding reception."

"Oh, a wedding reception. You're having a social life while I'm locked up here playing Florence Nightingale. Terrific. But tell me. What kind of miracle did he do? On second thought, don't bother. I figured it out myself: he took out the brain which you did have and put in a backbone which you didn't—making you stupid and stubborn all at once."

"You want to hear about this or not?" I snap at her. In my head, though, I get a funny idea she may be half right, so I laugh and say, "Okay make it two miracles: one on me and one with the wine."

"What wine?"

"Actually it was the water. You know those champagne fountains, where you pour the wine in the top and it runs out of four dolphins' mouths? Well, about halfway through the reception, Barbara—that's Jerry's mother—comes up to him and says they're out of champagne. He gives her a kind of short answer, but then he goes into the kitchen and I follow him. The place, of course, is knee deep in empties so he just tells one of the caterer's girls to fill them up with tap water and start dumping them in the fountain."

"You're going to tell me it actually came out champagne?"

"Not only champagne. Terrific champagne. What they had to start with was really not bad—Korbel Brut. But what came out after the water went in was like Piper Heidsieck at least. You should've heard the raves. The bride's father, of course, was so crocked he took credit for saving the best stuff till last—as if he'd bought it himself right from the start."

"I thought you said it was a miracle. You mean to say nobody connected it with Jerry at all? That's the dumbest thing so far."

"Not nobody. The waitress knew. And so did I and a couple of the other witnesses who were in the kitchen. That's about it though."

"You're telling me he does a parlor trick for a half dozen people and you call that a miracle?"

"That's what I'm telling you, Shirley. For me, it was evidence that I should trust him. For you, obviously, it's not enough. That's why I'm going to Cleveland and you're staying here."

At this point, I get a surprise. Rhoda, it turns out, has been standing in the hallway behind me, listening for I don't know how long. Besides all her other annoying habits, she moves like an Indian so you can never hear her coming. All of a sudden, though, she butts right in: "He really did that? Turned water into champagne? Does he also do miracles on people?"

"I suppose he could," I tell her. "It's just that I've never seen any. Some day, maybe. Who knows? By the way. You feeling any better?"

I have no intention of listening to her answer, so I reach over and help myself to another strawberry tart.

"No. Worse," she says. "If I'm not in the hospital on Monday, that'll really be a miracle. But tell me something. This Jerry. You think you could get him to come here? After all these doctors, I'm willing to try anything."

"Don't get your hopes up, Momma," Shirley pipes in with another zinger. "Marvin's friend Jerry is not only God, but a cook besides. Between the two, he probably couldn't fit you into his schedule."

"Don't be so smart, Shirley," Rhoda zings right back. "I wouldn't care of somebody claimed to be King Tut, as long as he could cure me. Listen though, I'm hungry. What is Marvin eating there?"

That's another thing about may mother-in-law that annoys the hell out of me: whenever she can, she asks Shirley the questions she should be asking me. This time, I don't let her get away with it. "Strawberry tarts, Rhoda," I tell her. "Also, some fantastic almond wafers. Jerry made them, as a matter of fact. And listen. In spite of what Shirley says, he's a very accommodating person. I can't see any reason why he couldn't come to New York some day."

By this time, Rhoda is sitting in the chair next to mine with the baked goods between us. For once, she doesn't say anything;

instead she just stares at the box. Finally, she says, "He actually made them? Himself?"

"Don't get any ideas, Momma," Shirley warns her. "I'll make you farina."

Rhoda, however, acts as if she doesn't hear her. "Tell me, Marvin," she says. "Could he do a miracle at a distance? On me, I mean?"

"I can't see why not," I say. "Tell you what. When I get back to Cleveland, I'll ask him."

"I didn't mean that," she says. "I meant right now."

"What? You want me to call him on the phone? He's hard to reach."

"No. I was just thinking. Maybe if I could have something he *touched*, it would work. Like one of those tarts, for instance."

"Momma!" Shirley shrieks. "They're *strawberry*! You might as well swallow a package of needles and get it over with."

"Shut up, Shirley," Rhoda says. "If they're miraculous tarts, how could they hurt you?"

"Listen Rhoda," I say, trying to slow her down. "I'm not so sure Shirley doesn't have a point. They're great tarts, but as far as I know, that's all they are."

"So what," she shoots back. "He made them, didn't he? I'm going to have one. And some cookies, too, for good measure."

She picks what she wants out of the box, but before she can take a bite, Shirley jumps up off the sofa and runs over to her.

"Momma, Momma," she says. "Look. I take back what I said. So maybe they are miraculous, okay? But why do you have to *eat* them? Maybe you could just rub them on yourself."

"That is the stupidest thing I ever heard, Shirley," Rhoda answers. "Baked goods are for eating. If God wanted me to rub something on, he would have showed up as a salve manufacturer, not a cook. Besides, the crumbs would itch me all night."

Once again, Rhoda doesn't notice the subject is getting away from her. I mean, when you think of what strawberry seeds could do to her insides, what's an itch? On the other hand, if the tarts were miraculous enough not to irritate her intestines, why would they bother her skin? Rhoda, however, does an end run around the whole subject and starts eating. "Very good," she says with her mouth full. "Pastry like this I haven't had for years. Reminds me of the Swiss bakery that used to be on Elmhurst Avenue in Queens. That man made apple pies that actually had crunchy sugar on the inside of the bottom crust."

By this time she's into the wafers, and Shirley is balancing on the thin edge between murder and tears. As I said, I'm not an unsympathetic person, so I get up and try to keep her from falling either way by giving her a little hug. "Look," I say. "I'm sorry about this, but it really wasn't my idea. Let's not get ahead of ourselves. With a little luck, maybe it won't bother her."

Shirley, of course, shakes herself loose from me and loses her balance both ways at once. "It's all your fault," she screams through her tears. "If she dies, I'll kill you!"

She runs out of the room and slams the bedroom door. Rhoda, by now, is on her second tart, so I figure the least I can do is get the rest away from her. "You mind if I have some more?" I ask her, taking the box over to the sofa. "They really are good, but I hope you haven't done yourself any harm by eating them. We worry about you, you know."

"Not anymore, you won't," she announces. "I'll just finish what I have here and go to bed. In the morning, I'll be all better. You watch."

"I really hope so, Rhoda," I say to her—because if she isn't, I think to myself, everybody's going to be one helluva lot worse.

She goes off and I just sit there. I'll get to what happened the next morning in a minute, but I have to tell you something I thought of for the first time that night. People talk as if faith was some kind of virtue which, if you have it, everybody else is going to turn blue with admiration. In fact, faith is almost always indistinguishable from stupidity. At least, there's absolutely no way you can convince anybody that they should have it. And what's more, when you do actually decide to trust somebody yourself, you should never even think of bragging about it. For all you know, you may just be ignoring a whole lot of things that any intelligent person would have seen right away.

What I mean is that, up to that night, I always thought trusting Jerry made at least some kind of sense. For me, at least. You know: *I'd* thought it through; *I'd* figured the risks; *I* knew what I was doing. But watching Rhoda made me wonder. What she was doing was just plain nuts; but how was I all that different? As far as Shirley was concerned, we both should've been committed. Ha! Faith! Maybe that's why they call it commitment.

Anyway, when I woke up in the morning, Shirley was still asleep, so I tiptoed out. Also, on my way down the hall, I checked Rhoda's door. It was closed and everything was quiet, but I hated to think what that might mean, so I just kept going. I figured I could use a little time by myself before the ceiling fell in again.

When I got to the living room though, the first thing I hear is Rhoda's voice coming from the kitchen. "Sit down, Marvin," she says. "Wait till you see what I've got for you."

"Are you all right?" I call to her. "I mean, with the strawberries and all?"

"I told you it would work," she says, coming into the room with a tray on which is coffee, juice, bagels and cream cheese. "Tell your friend Jerry he cured me completely. And thank him for me. And ask him how soon I can come to Cleveland and meet him. Right now though, have a little breakfast. I made it specially for you."

Talk about mixed emotions: I'm glad she thinks she's cured; I'm dying to talk about it with Jerry; I'm terrified at the thought of having Rhoda on my hands in Cleveland; I'm touched as hell that for the first time in my life she's serving me anything; and, having tasted what she calls coffee, I'm trying to think of an excuse to have just juice. Like a dope, though, all I say is, "You really think you're cured?"

As I say this, I'm holding half a bagel in my left hand and aiming a knife at the cream cheese with my right. Rhoda is standing in front of my chair. "I don't *think* I'm cured," she announces. "I know it! Look!"

Right in front of my face, she waves the paper folder with the two squares on it. "See?" she says. "No blue. A little brown, but that you have to expect. The background is pure white."

Needless to say, I nearly throw up. I drop both the bagel and the knife and by the time I get her to put the testing thing away, I can't eat even a mouthful. Still, I manage to carry on a conversation with her till Shirley gets up, after which I get dressed and go for a long walk.

The rest of the weekend was pretty good. Rhoda seemed actually cured, even though she still couldn't get off the subject of her insides, and Shirley was only feisty instead of nasty. And I myself finally learned something: Jerry was absolutely right about the stupidity of trying to fix up the world by miracles. A whole new creation is what it needs, not tinkering. It was nice, of course, that Rhoda got over her diverticulitis. But on any reasonable view of things, her intestines were a pretty dumb place to stop overhauling her. For openers at least, the job should have included a little work on her mouth so she wouldn't keep carrying on about bowel movements while people are eating—and on her head, for that matter, to stop her from thinking she should boil coffee till it tastes like acid.

But—and this is what Jerry used to say, too—if you just diddle with the world like that, all you end up doing is changing so many things, one at a time, that finally not even God could remember what it was you started out to fix. All at once really is the only way. The hard part for me, of course, was to stop wishing I could have both a backbone *and* a brain while I was waiting.

6

I left for Cleveland sooner than I thought. Sunday night turned out to be practically a talkathon, what with Rhoda trying to sell me on the idea of letting her come along and Shirley trying to talk me out of going at all. After they ran out of steam and finally went to bed, I called the airline and changed to a Monday morning flight.

When I started telling you this story, I thought that once I got to the part where I was in Cleveland for good it'd be easy. Now that I try to organize it though, it refuses to stay the same twice in a row. That's partly, I suppose, because I still haven't sorted it all out myself. But mostly I think it's because all through the rest of the time I spent with Jerry, he kept giving off two different sets of signals about what he was up to.

The first set was his no-miracles, "all at once is the only way" pitch—which also included, though not often and never in public, his actually claiming to be God. When he was on that track, he sounded as if he'd never do another cure again. "What's the point of tearing around confusing everybody with Band Aid jobs," he'd say, "when I'm going to cure them all in one shot just by dying and rising? People think it would be neat to have a divine physician, but they never stop to figure the drawbacks. For one thing, they'd swamp him with work—a rash at 9:00 A.M., a throat condition at 9:05, a hemorrhoid at 9:15—besides trampling each other to death trying to get to him. What's worse, half of them wouldn't settle for just a miraculous G.P. They'd insist on a divine dermatologist, a divine ENT man, even a divine proctologist . . . which has got to be a new low, even for God jokes."

On the other hand, there were lots of times he acted as if he thought miracles were exactly what the doctor ordered. Even though doing them made him grouchy, all anybody had to do was hand him a sob story and he came right through with a cure. We'd try every now and then to stop them from coming, but he'd just say, "Don't give them a hard time. At least they know they're not going to make it on their own—which is more than you can say for the Pentagon crowd, for example." The trouble was, neither one of the two sets of signals ever completely won out.

Oh, I suppose in a way the dying and rising angle sort of did. After he actually made good on it, he not only didn't do any more cures, he didn't stay around to do anything. But even though that was what he said he'd do all along, there never seemed to be any systematic progress toward it. I mean, you'd have expected maybe that most of the miracles would have come early on, and that later they would get phased out in favor of the death talk. As it was though, both things were always there: on any given day he could shift back and forth between them a dozen times.

That's what makes the story so hard to tell. Even though it does fall into two parts (before and after the weird thing that happened on August sixth)—and even though he did dwell more on dying in the second part—he kept doing cures right up to the end. So when I try to pinpoint anything, I'm never a hundred percent sure which miracle, or which lecture against miracles, goes where. I know I've got what he said and did pretty much right; but I can't guarantee I've got everything where it actually happened. What I'm saying, in other words, is that the sequences I end up giving you might sometimes be more Marvin than Jerry. It probably doesn't matter all that much, though: he had a way of getting through regardless.

Maybe I should begin with a general impression first. I'm a person who's used to living out of a suitcase, but being with Jerry was something else: he made floating around an art form. Maybe it was the generation gap. If you turned twenty-one in the fifties like I did, you like a little dependability, not to mention privacy, in your life. With these kids, though (and I include Jerry, because he grew up in the sixties when being a teenager went from a phase to a career), not only did you just "hang out" and "crash"; nobody was ever alone for a minute.

In a way, it was unfair. Jerry went off by himself whenever he felt like it, which was a lot, but the rest of us were always stuck with each other. If he was around, we were together because we felt we should be with him, and if he wasn't, we just stayed together comparing notes and generally getting on each other's nerves.

For instance, I almost always ended up bunking with Curtis Brock—an arrangement which, considering his sexual preferences and mine, was not exactly the match of the century. Not that I slept with my eyes open or anything: he never gave even a hint of being on the make as far as I was concerned. As a matter of fact, being gay didn't give him nearly the problems that being smart did.

He could talk circles around anybody. In fact, apart from Jerry, there was only one in the whole group who was any kind of match for him. That was Greg Waters. But since Curtis definitely had a jealously problem with him—and since Greg was so wrapped up in Jerry he never gave Curtis the time of day—the two of them had as little to do with each other as possible. That left Curtis pretty much with only me to spend his time with: I was, after all, at least the third-ranking talker in the crowd, besides being his own age and no threat to whatever he thought was his relationship with Jerry.

In any case, no matter how it all fell apart later on, I have to say that most of what I finally did understand about Jerry I owe to Curtis. He was the only one who really thought through the dying and rising business. It was a little ghoulish, in fact, how enthusiastic he could be about it. "It's absolutely elegant," he would say. "The only thing anybody needs is the one thing everybody has: death. The new order gets them all at once by a single device." So much so, that every time Jerry started doing miracles again or talking about how people should prepare themselves for the new order, Curtis would carry on about what he called "this compromising of everything." It was almost as if it was his own brainchild. Everything else in the world was allowed to die, but not his bright idea about dying. Still, as I said, I owe him. It was just too bad it had to work out the way it did.

But that's getting way ahead of the story, so let me go back to the lifestyle with Jerry. The word that keeps coming to me to describe it is "free," but in a lot of ways it wasn't. For one thing, none of us felt free to leave, even though supposedly we could've any time we liked. That bothered me a lot. I mean, think about what I just said: it sounds exactly like those people who get involved with sects. Here I am, I would think to myself, a middle-aged guy. Have I been conned? Should I get myself deprogrammed before I end up with my head shaved, passing out pamphlets in an airport?

Mostly, though, it wasn't that bad: for the first time in my life I really was doing something I wanted to do. But "free" still wasn't exactly the word for it: it was costing me a bundle. Curtis and I sat down one night and figured out what the two of us had poured into six months of hanging around with Jerry. It came to some $30,000—$20,000 of it mine and the rest his. Where'd it all go? Well, one thing about Jerry: he had absolutely no qualms about spending other people's money. If you had anything less than a miser's grip on it, he'd pry it loose and blow it.

One day, for instance, he decided we'd been roughing it too long: we needed, he said, "a civilized meal for a change." At the time, we were staying in an inner city walkup with some friends of his, so around noontime he strolls in and says, "Marvin let's do a little shopping for supper." Naturally, I expect to spring for the grocery bill, but the first place he takes me is a restaurant supply. "Did you get a look at that kitchen where we're staying, Marvin?" he asks me. "It's ridiculous. Three hopeless pots, and not a decent knife in the place." I tell him all they do is heat up Spaghetti-o's, but he's not listening. Instead, he starts pulling stuff off the shelves and piling it on the counter: a 20-quart pot that costs $95—and which shocks me so completely I don't even take in the prices on all the pans, knives, strainers and cutting boards. Only the whole bill, which I'll never forget: $410.75.

After that, we hit a couple of fancy grocery stores and a butcher shop where he drops sixty more of my dollars on veal he claims is "too good to pass up." Finally, we go for wine. Red, he thinks he'd like, from California. I ask him if I should grab a couple of jugs of

Gallo, but he's already got his eye on what he wants. It's called Cakebox or Breadcake or something: "Hey," he crows across the store, "this is the 1978! It's terrific! If they've got a case, we should buy it." Naturally, they have, and we do: to the tune of another $135.

He cooked just the one meal with all that stuff. The hardware, plus the food and wine that was left over, he left behind for the people in the apartment. Still, it was when he did things like that, especially with my money, that I got a real feeling of freedom. To most people, money is some kind of holy thing. They get practically reverent about holding onto it, and if they do actually part with some, right away they want to be reassured they didn't do something sacrilegious like not getting their money's worth.

Jerry though, went out of his way "to rattle the true believers' cages," as he put it. He didn't usually smoke, but every now and then he'd light a cigarette with a fifty dollar bill. The first time he did that—with one of my fifties, naturally—I nearly died. But he just said, "See, Marvin? All this time you were embarrassed you didn't have religion. You have as much as anybody. Now all you have to do is figure out a way to get rid of it."

And I did too, pretty much. After a while, I got almost as big a kick out of thumbing my nose at the system as he did. Sometimes he would help people, not with miracles the way they expected, but just by giving them money—especially if he could get somebody else to do the giving. Once, when he'd talked me into giving five hundred to some completely questionable character, there was this social worker type who tried to tell me you can't solve peoples' problems by throwing money at them. "I don't know about that," I told her. "At least it beats throwing sociology. Besides, even if it doesn't help the throwee, it has a hell of a liberating effect on the thrower. You give *me* five hundred and we'll all be happy."

Another time, though, Jerry did something that was both a miracle and a slap at money at once. He'd run up a bunch of bills buying things for various people and, after about three dunnings, the biggest creditor started threatening him. "Well, Marvin," he says, "I guess we'd better settle, huh?" I'm short of cash, however, due to my partner being late with a payment, so I tell him unfortunately he's out of luck. I start to say that if he can stall for a week more maybe . . . but he just smiles and says I should forget it and go buy a Perdue Oven Stuffer for supper.

Well, when I bring it home, he says to me, "Stick around a minute Marvin; I'll show you something even Frank Perdue doesn't know." Then he slices open the plastic wrapper, puts the chicken down on the counter, pulls out the paper that has the neck and so forth in it, and starts this line of patter about what's inside it. "You talk about miracles, Marvin," he says. "The chicken business is full of them. This bird, for example, has two necks, half a heart and three livers. Probably a big talker, a lousy lover and a heavy drinker. It's a miracle it grew up at all." Then he rummages around in the wrapper again and pulls out what looks like a soggy cigar butt. "Here," he says, handing it to me. "Maybe you should pay those bills before Mr. Perdue misses this." I unroll the thing: it's ten $100 bills. "Hey," I say, "how'd . . . ?" "Never mind, Marvin," he says. "Now I'm going to show you something really important: watch me and you'll learn the world's best way to truss a chicken."

7

W hat I just told you about Jerry and money is a perfect example of the way my mind gets things out of sequence. I start talking about a dinner party Jerry threw in early March and I jump right away to his pulling the thousand dollars out of the chicken, which he didn't do until after August sixth. I'd apologize, but since this seems to be the only way I can tell the story, I'm not going to worry about it anymore.

I don't want to give you the impression that Jerry just larked around doing miracles and making wisecracks. As a matter of fact, he spent most of his time in public talking about the new order—a subject about which he was as serious as Spencer ever was, but in a different way. When Spencer talked about it, two things hit you. One was that he was negative as hell: the old order, whether it was the government, or the arms race, or money, or the threat to the environment, was nothing but bad news. But the other thing was that even when he did occasionally make a positive suggestion, it never made you feel very hopeful. As I told you, he'd urge people to renounce the evils of the system, but since his audiences were 60 percent kids and the rest pretty much losers, you got the distinct feeling the whole effort was wasted. Nobody who had any real influence over the system was even there.

With Jerry though—if you could ever get yourself to the point of trusting him to deliver on what he was promising—you didn't feel hopeless at all. It was interesting. Spencer's remedies made sense. You know, stop the arms buildup, stop wrecking the ecology; but they didn't have the chances of soup in a sieve since people's good intentions just drained out through the holes in their heads. What Jerry talked about, on the other hand, made practically no sense at all, but somehow you felt relieved. He never said the new order would come if people straightened up and flew right; he said it was already in the works and all they had to do was trust it. In other words, he talked as if the real remedies hardly depended on their cooperation at all. It was like if you had a cold. He didn't tell you to take two aspirin and call him in the morning; he made you believe it was already morning now.

Maybe that's a dumb illustration, but it's exactly the kind of thing Jerry used to say. He always talked in comparisons. His were better than that, of course, but he practically never talked about anything serious in a straight way. His illustrations seemed straightforward enough when you first heard them—a lot of them, in fact, were taken right out of his experience as a cook; but after you thought about them for a while, they could raise more questions than they answered.

For instance. He said the new order was like yeast in bread dough: without it the dough would just be a lump of paste that, if you tried to bake it, would turn into an inedible rock. But with the yeast mixed in, the whole thing was transformed into something light and delicious.

You may think that sounds simple, but it's not. Most people, when they heard it, assumed that the yeast stood for some special dose of Spencer-type good deeds which, if they could manage to inject them into the old order, would turn it into the new one. I thought so myself for a long time but eventually I realized Jerry hadn't meant that at all. He meant that the whole new order was the yeast, and that since it was already completely distributed all through the lump of the old order, all you had to do was trust it and wait. Nobody had to do a thing to activate it; it did all the work by itself.

When I finally caught on to that, it sounded like the first piece of good news I ever heard. Crazy, maybe; farfetched, probably; also unlikely, for all I knew. But definitely not the bad news that everybody else was peddling in the name of hope. Lots of people, though, had fits about it. They'd carry on about how that was de-meaning to people, how it gave them nothing to do but wait. To me that was a pretty stupid objection, since just waiting would be a hell of an improvement over most of the things they were likely to do instead, like making bigger and better missiles, or carting their toxic wastes off to somebody else's backyard. But they went right on complaining that Jerry was encouraging passivity and moral in-difference.

It never seemed to bother him, though. If he answered them at all, it was just with another comparison. I remember once when he was using the yeast illustration, some guy got up and insisted on being told what he ought to do to help the new order along. Jerry looked at him for a while as if he was having a hard time understanding; then he said, "Well, I suppose there are two things you could try. The first is, since you're not a yeast plant, don't waste any time trying to mix yourself into the old order: human beings just suffocate in the conditions that yeast thrives under. The second is, since you're about to get a loaf of fresh bread in a couple of hours, why not just go get yourself some wine and cheese?"

That was typical. Not that it satisfied the guy with the ques-tion. The thing about Jerry was that if you could bring yourself to trust him personally, you thought his answers were terrific; but if you couldn't, they pissed you off. That's why, when people asked me to explain Jerry's teaching about the new order, I almost never had any hope of getting it across to them. Not only did he make it a mysterious, hidden thing, like yeast, he also made it inseparable from himself. Somehow, the whole process of fixing up everything that was wrong with the world was already at work—and already finished, in fact—inside him.

What illustrates that best is the connection he always made between the new order and his personal rising from the dead. In a minute I'll tell you something that shows it perfectly, but first I should be honest with you. Now that the whole business is finished and he's really risen, I find it easy to act as if I was always a hundred percent convinced he could actually bring it off. But I wasn't. In fact, even though he talked about dying and rising lots of times before he did—and even though he went as far as to raise other people from the dead—I have to admit that right up to the last, I was always at least a little skeptical. Either I hedged my bets and thought, well, we'll just have to see, won't we? Or else I didn't think about it at all. So keep that in mind while I'm telling you this story: most of my conclusions about it came after it was over. While it was happening, my mind was almost as much a blank as anybody's.

But back to the business about the new order being already at work in the world. One night very soon after I got to Cleveland for good, Jerry was talking to this big crowd, when all of a sudden a well-dressed man walks straight up to him, falls down on his knees and starts asking him will he come and do a miracle on his daughter who is dying in a hospital six blocks away. So what does Jerry do? Well, like I said, one sob story and up he comes with a new set of plans for the evening: off we all go to the hospital just like that. On foot, yet.

The crowd, needless to say, is confused by this, but not so much that they break up. Most of them follow right along, making a scene that looks like a low-budget version of the storming of the Bastille. Then suddenly in the midst of all the pushing and shoving Jerry stops dead in his tracks and looks annoyed. "Somebody touched me," he growls. Obviously, nobody knows what to say since at least twenty people a minute have been bumping into him for three blocks. But he just repeats, "I know somebody touched me. I lost power."

Once again, this does not exactly explain things to anybody, but he just stands there with the crowd getting quieter and quieter until finally, right in back of him, there comes this woman's voice.

"Please," she says. "Don't be angry. I only touched your sweatshirt, and I'm sorry if I bothered you—but it's cured, I think."

"What's cured?" Jerry asks her.

"My . . . hemorrhaging," she says. "I've had it twelve years. Now, one tug on your shirt and it's gone. It's a miracle. How can I thank you?"

Jerry looks at her in amazement. "Why should you thank a

cafeteria counter? If you got what you wanted, thank yourself."
Then he smiles and says, "Seriously, I'm glad it was there. But if
you'll excuse me now, I have to go see this man's daughter."

When we get to the hospital, of course, we lose most of the
crowd either outside or at the desk, but since it still looks like half
a mob scene, Jerry says only the father of the girl, plus the two
Waters kids and myself, should go up to her room. Why the Waters
boys, you ask? Well, this again is typical of Jerry—and of the not
fantastically neat situations he was always a kind of a magnet for.
The girl's father it turns out, is the current boyfriend of Greg's and
Timmy's mother who, naturally, is already in the hall outside the
room as we arrive—along with the girl's mother, as well as a couple
of grandmothers and aunts I never did get sorted out.

As you can imagine, it is not the friendliest looking group on
earth. At the time we arrive, though, they're all at least doing the
same thing, namely, crying like Niagara because the girl is already
dead. Between sobs, of course, they manage to get in a few remarks
about how the father might at least have been there for the death if
he hadn't been off pestering some useless miracle worker, but Jerry
just ignores them. "It's okay," he says. "Not to worry. She's not
dead; she's just asleep."

Well, if you know anything about people, you know that in a
group like that there's a lot of loose hostility looking for somebody
to zero in on. What they do is go straight from tears to snotty remarks about who made him a specialist and what makes him think
he knows more than the nurse who said she was dead ten minutes
ago and went to get the resident to pronounce it official? Once
again, Jerry just says, "Let me go in anyway. If I can't wake her up,
I'll be the first to admit it."

I take this as a signal to do something, so while Jerry is still
talking to the bunch in the hall, I open the door to the girl's room
and take Greg, Timmy and her father inside with me. The four of
us walk straight over to the bed, and since it still takes Jerry a good
thirty seconds to catch up with us, we just stand there and stare at
her.

In what I'm going to tell you next, it's important to pay attention to exactly what happened when. As I said, at the time I didn't understand it all; but I thought a lot about it afterwards and I came to the conclusion that in this particular case, the sequence is the clue to the whole thing. Look at it: When the four of us get into the room, the girl is dead. The nurse, who was an old pro, was sure of it ten minutes ago. The rest of us, who spend thirty seconds just staring at her, don't see a single sign of life: not a flutter of an eyelid, not a breath of any kind. Then Jerry comes into the room. But he doesn't come all the way over to the bed at first: for some reason he pauses for about three beats just inside the doorway. But right in that pause, the girls starts breathing again: quietly but obviously, exactly as if suddenly she really was asleep instead of dead—making us all wonder, of course, if Jerry wasn't right all along.

In any case, when he gets to the bedside he certainly acts as if he was. He just takes her hand, pats it and says, "C'mon, kid, time to wake up." Then, nice as you please, she gives a little twitch, yawns, rubs her eyes and sits straight up in the bed. When the bunch in the hall find this out, of course, they come bursting in, scaring her half back to death or whatever. And, true to form, they touch all the nasty bases they can find: the nurse should be fired for spreading false rumors; Jerry just had the dumb luck to walk in after a mistake; if the father wasn't fooling around on the side, the kid would probably never have gotten sick in the first place. Jerry tunes it all out and picks up the phone instead. "This is room 227," he says. "We'd like a grilled cheese with bacon and a large Coke. Quick too. After what this girl's been through, she needs nourishment."

I think you probably see what I'm getting at in all this, but let me spell it out anyway. These were two very funny miracles. So much so, in fact, that I wouldn't even call them such. As far as I can see, Jerry didn't *do* anything in either case. The woman with the hemorrhaging just sort of helped herself to something that was already available—almost cafeteria-style, as Jerry said. He was as ignorant of what ailment she had—and of what she thought she was doing, and of how she was actually cured—as anybody else in the crowd.

But it's the dead girl that's the clincher. She came back to life, not because Jerry *did* something to her, but because his *presence*—his just being there inside the door to her room—*had that effect on her.* In other words, it goes back to what I was saying about the new order being already present and already at work in him: health and life—and, if I'm right, everything else about the new order—were simply *there,* for the asking, wherever he was. And not even for the asking, really—because the girl, obviously, was in no condition to ask for a thing. It was all just there, as he said, like yeast. All you had to do was wait for it to do its own thing and eventually you'd have bread. Not to mention, I suppose, cheese, bacon and a Coke.

In any case, the net result of the scene in the hospital was that except for those of us who were in the room when she started breathing again—and for Curtis, whom I'll tell you about in a minute—nobody gave Jerry credit for a miracle at all. And even as far as we were concerned, it still didn't seem like a particularly orthodox one, if there is such a thing. When something happens while a person looks like he isn't doing anything at all, it takes you a while before you figure out a connection.

When I told Curtis about it though, he put a typical double whammy on himself. His first reaction, when I said Jerry didn't obviously do anything to the girl, was to recognize right away that it still had to be a miracle. He explained it pretty much the way I just did, but at the time, the explanation went right over my head. His second reaction, however, was to get mad at Jerry for going into the hospital room at all. "Sometimes I wonder, Marvin," he fumed, "whether Jerry understands his own message. Raising people prematurely like that—especially raising them one by one—just confuses the issue. The last thing in the world it will suggest to them is that the new order is a universal mystery that works through death. All they'll think is that Jerry's in the world to do the very patch jobs on the old order he supposedly disapproves of."

And he doesn't let it go at that, either. Curtis being Curtis, he decides it's his responsibility to deliver this dressing-down to Jerry in person. And without a whole lot of regard, I might add, for who he's supposedly straightening out. I know; I was there. He starts out calmly enough, trying to explain how raising dead people ahead of time obscures everything. But then when Jerry just more or less agrees with him, he takes this as permission to act like an agent reading the riot act to a performer who's been doing gigs in the wrong places. "All right," he says. "Since we're agreed, please try a little harder to stay away from death and dying. That means no more hospitals, and especially no more emergency rooms . . ." (Jerry had already raised one kid right as they were moving him out of the ER to the morgue) ". . . and above all, it means you don't go to any funerals whatsoever."

All Jerry said was, "Right, Curtis." His tone was agreeable enough, but somehow he struck me as a little sad. I didn't make anything of it at the time: like so many things—including especially the whole relationship between Jerry and Curtis—I just filed it away in the back of my mind. As I see it now, though, Jerry must've known or at least suspected all along that Curtis was going to be the cause of his death; but since he apparently didn't know exactly how, he just never talked about it. Instead, he almost always said yes to anything Curtis suggested—leaving the little sadness as the only hint he gave that he thought anything was wrong.

I'll give you one more example of Curtis's agent routine. Quite often, especially when he first began talking about the new order in public, Jerry would sound almost exactly like Spencer. You know: he would say that people ought to get ready for it by straightening up their acts, by making protests—even by writing congressmen. To me, this didn't seem like a particularly horrible thing to do. I mean, even if it wasn't going to have anymore effect than Spencer's programs had had, it at least got them a little critical of the old order and a little enthusiastic about the new one.

Jerry apparently thought that way, too. Once, when Curtis was complaining to him about how his public talks sounded like "no advance whatsoever over Spencer's self-improvement schemes," Jerry actually defended them a little. "What's the harm, Curtis?" he said. "If you're eventually going to give everybody in the world the free gift of a fantastic wine cellar, why is it such a terrible idea to tell them they should stop drinking cream soda in the meantime? When the wine finally arrives, they might actually have a clue what to do with it."

Curtis, though, always had an answer. "The harm is," he said, as if he was explaining something to a not-too-bright kid, "that the clue you're talking about is practically the last thing in the world that will occur to them. In all likelihood, since they can only *believe* in the gift of the wine, while they can actually *experience* the absence of cream soda, the first conclusion they'll come to is that you've made abstinence from soda not only the *condition* of the gift but also the *cause* of it. They might even, for all you know, decide that abstinence is the ideal way to deal with the wine when they finally get it. All of which, obviously, is exactly 180 degrees off the mark."

Predictably, Jerry just smiles his sad smile and agrees with him. "I guess you're right, Curtis," he says. "No more speeches about what people ought to do to get ready. Fair enough?" He even went out of his way to invent an illustration of Curtis's point right there on the spot. "You know what it's like? Trying to give people advice, I mean. It's like redoing a kitchen. You tell them all the new equipment they should have, and where everything should go for the best work flow, and it sounds terrific. Actually, though, there's no way they can ever put it into practice because when they finally start dealing with the kitchen they now have, it turns out that it has an impossible shape, the floor needs shoring up, and all the plumbing is in the wrong places. In other words, even if they accept the plan you suggested, when they finally take a good look from the inside at what it's going to cost them to tear it all down, ninety-nine percent of them will just give up. So it does very little good to tell them things like, 'Stop fouling up the environment,' or, 'Make love, not war,' or even something as apparently doable as, 'Feed the hungry.' If they spent what it would take to clean up their factory, the stockholders would have their necks for cutting into the dividends; if they made love, half of it would still be indistinguishable from war anyway; and even if they sent food to the hungry, most of it would end up on the black market. Good advice just takes their minds off the fact that the only way they can possibly fix anything is to tear down the selves that messed it up in the first place."

You'd think that when Jerry gets done handing Curtis this illustration, it would be the end of the smart-agent-dumb-performer routine for a while. But it wasn't. Curtis, of course, has more sense than to stay miffed when he's agreed with. But even so, he still can't stop giving advice. So what if Jerry just drew him the picture he asked for? Right away Curtis has to tell him how to put a better point on his pencil. "That's marvelous," he says, "but don't you see where you can go from there? From the part about tearing down themselves, I mean: the demolition that's necessary for the new order comes to them gratis in the death that's the only requirement for the new order. They don't have to find it; it finds them. The whole thing is absolutely elegant."

Again, Jerry just smiled. I myself had a different reaction: I swore that if I had to listen to Curtis say the word "elegant" once more, I'd scream.

8

As far as I can tell, there were two turning points in Jerry's thinking—two steps, sort of, by which he went from talking about dying and rising as just an eventuality, to actually becoming aware it was something that would happen to him sooner than later.

The first one came in late May. He'd been talking publicly about the new order for about six months by then and, as I told you, he'd done a lot of miraculous cures. At the beginning, he drew only small crowds, but as his reputation for being a wonderworker got around, all he had to do was come out of hiding and mobs of people showed up. This particular time, it was a beautiful warm spring day and, having gotten up late, he decided around noon just to go out and enjoy the weather for a couple of hours in the park.

Well, first thing you know, some people recognize him and begin hanging around, so he just starts talking quietly as usual. Pretty soon though, since it's lunch hour, the place is jammed with people and Jerry is standing up on a park bench, going on full blast about the slavery of the old order and the freedom of the new—especially from the religion of money.

One thing about Jerry when he got on that subject: he really made people laugh at themselves. I remember that day in particular, he started talking to this junior executive type in the front of the crowd. "Suppose I asked you," he says to him, "to give me a tenth of your paycheck every week: what would you say?"

The guy laughs once and in a good-natured way says, "I'd say you were crazy. I'm already hanging by a short rope. You want me to make it even shorter?"

Quick as a flash, Jerry picks up on him: "Listen, if your feet aren't touching the floor now, hanging six inches higher is hardly going to be a tragedy." Then off he goes with the illustration: how the essence of the money religion is to keep everybody's feet off the floor so they'll always be scheming to get more rope and scared to death of giving any away; how all the time the only thing the rope is doing is choking them; and finally, how if they do manage to get a little more rope, all that happens is that somebody lowers the floor on them and they're still hanging. "You claim you couldn't take a one-tenth cut in your income without it ruining you," he says to him. "Listen, since 1960, you've had a hundred percent raise. Whatever happened to that? You're lucky if your real income is off by only a tenth. At least if you cut your own salary by giving some away, you get the pleasure of beating the system to the punch."

In any case, by about 1:30 when it was time for everybody to go back to work, he had them feeling so liberated that hardly any of them left. The crowd grew, in fact, so that by 3:30, when Jerry's voice finally gave out, there had to be about five thousand people in the park. And since after that he just started talking to individuals again and actually doing cures on the ones who were sick, nobody left then either. The net result was that the afternoon turned into a kind of picnic without food. The two or three hot dog vendors that happened to be there were cleaned out early, after which they also took the day off and lolled around on the grass like everybody else. Even the cures seemed kind of relaxed: no jamming up of people in front of Jerry, just everybody waiting till it seemed time and then quietly going up to him. Very orderly. Best-natured bunch of people I ever saw.

This went on till almost 8:00 when, for no apparent reason except maybe tiredness, there's suddenly a lull in things. Jerry stretches out flat on the park bench, puts his hands behind his head and stares at the sky, which is starting to get dark. "You know," he says, "this is a terrific crowd. Too bad we haven't got anything to feed them. Pizza would be nice. Wine, too."

There were only a couple of us close to him at that point and I just thought he was relaxing and letting his mind drift, which

I'm sure he was. Beth Murphy, though, for some reason takes him seriously. "That's impossible," she says. "You know what even one slice of pizza each would cost? At $6.00 a pie, that's 75 cents a slice, that's like $3,750.00, without wine."

My brother Howie is also sitting there and since he can never resist kidding, he says to Beth, "There's a girl on the other side of the fence over there walking a pizza home. Maybe if you could get her to slice it real thin, everybody could have at least a flake of oregano."

She starts to complain he's being ridiculous, but suddenly Jerry sits up on the bench and cuts her off. "Hey, that's not a bad idea," he says to me. "Marvin, go over and invite her in. Ask her if she'll loan us her pizza for about twenty minutes."

Naturally, I still assume he's fooling around, but I go anyway. The girl is maybe fifteen and about as soft as a fistful of carpet tacks. I ask her would she like to come in and she wants to know what it's worth to me.

"No, no," I tell her, "it's not that. We'd just like to borrow your pizza for a while."

"That's a new one," she says. "Listen, I don't give it away and I don't lend it. Especially to bunches of guys. Who's 'we' anyway?"

"Me and my friends over there," I tell her. "And seriously, it's not what you think. We just want to use . . ." (it takes me I don't know how many tries before I come up with a word she can't take two ways) ". . . your . . . I mean . . . the . . . food you're carrying . . . for a few minutes. Don't worry . . . nobody's going to touch you."

She ignores this, and peers over at the bench. "Hey," she says. "Is the cute guy in the sweatshirt one of your friends?"

I say, "Sure. In fact, he's the one who wants to borrow your . . ." And once again, I pull myself up short.

"In that case, I'll take it over myself," she says. "But what's he mean, 'borrow'? You guys making a movie or something? He the director? Would he put me in it?"

"You'll have to ask him" I say. "But thanks, anyway. It's very nice of you."

"Hunhh," she shrugs as we start walking toward the nearest

gate. "Least it beats going home and listening to my father freak out about how his pizza's cold 'cause I stood around talking to guys. And besides, I got anchovy, which he hates. What's your friend's name, Pops?"

"Jerry," I tell her, and walk her over to the bench feeling about ninety. When we get there, though, Jerry apparently doesn't notice. He just thanks the girl, pouring on the charm, and tells me to go round up the rest of the witnesses so we can hand the pizza out.

Once again, I do what I'm told without knowing what I'm doing. When I get them all around him, he slips the string off the box, flips back the lid and starts handing out slices two at a time. "Pass them around," he says. "Let's see how far we can stretch this."

I get the first two pieces and either the girl is a chronic liar or something funny is up, because they're so hot I can hardly hold onto them. Also, on my way back for more, I see at least seven of us witnesses carrying slices out and when I get back to Jerry, I notice there's still a whole pie in the box. By now, the scene is like a bucket brigade in a silent movie and stays that way for almost half an hour: out of the box, pass them along, out of the box, pass them along, till everybody is full and saying, "No more, please."

Finally, I turn to Jerry to tell him I think that about does it, but he's in some kind of trance and I have to say it three times. When he finally catches on, he stares at the box for a minute before he closes it up. When he hands it back to the girls, he says, "See? I told you we only wanted to borrow it: one sausage pizza for your father, good as new. Thanks again."

Needless to say, little Miss Mouth is not quite so quick with the words this time. In fact, she gets one feel of the heat coming out of the bottom of the box and practically runs out of the park. Jerry looks at her for a minute and then turns to me. "Tell them to pick up all the crusts, Marvin," he says, sounding tired. "Then you guys go on back to the house. After I say goodbye to the crowd, I think I'm going to need a little time by myself."

Well, they picked up the place and filled every park department basket in sight with pizza crusts. By that time, it was pretty obvious to everybody what had happened. At the start, of course, people just assumed the slices were being passed out from someplace in the middle of the crowd where a whole lot of pizzas had been delivered. But as the word got around that Jerry had fed the whole bunch of them with just one pie, they started calling it the biggest miracle ever and saying that Jerry ought to be mayor of Cleveland, if not President of the United States.

That, I think, is what made the feeding of the crowd the first of the two turning points I mentioned to you. Up to then he just thought that people *might* take his miracles as a substitute for his message; after that though, the "might" disappeared in favor of "would." He was finally convinced that *any* miracle he did would be practically guaranteed to give people the wrong impression. Not that he hadn't said as much all along. And not that his miracles were all that flashy and attention-getting: most of them, in fact, were sort of laid back. I mean, take the pizza for five thousand. There wasn't one bit of hocus-pocus about it: he just kept passing out slices that just kept on being there to be passed out. Not only that, but like a good three-fourths of his miracles, it hardly even seemed intentional on his part. As I said, it was as if the feeding and the cures and the raisings just came out of him because of what other people wanted.

In any case though, every time he did one, their attention to the new order—and especially to any mention of his dying—was short-circuited: all they could imagine by way of a program for him was more and more patchwork miracles. And after the one with the pizza—especially since he did it on a day when he'd talked for three hours about the mess the old order was in—they got really serious about trying to put him in some position where he could do his miracles on a grand scale. The talk about mayor and president wasn't just hot air: if he hadn't gotten away from that crowd, sure as hell somebody would have organized something.

Still, he did get away—farther away, as a matter of fact, than anybody, including us witnesses, was prepared for. It's practically a story in itself. As I told you, he'd sent us back to the house and gone off somewhere by himself after he said goodbye to the crowd. So naturally, since that was around 9:00 P.M., we don't particularly think about him for a while. Finally, though, somebody notices it's after midnight and we begin wondering a little. At 1:00, in fact, Howie goes over to the park to check, but he comes back saying the place is deserted and he can't find Jerry anywhere. I for one begin to get concerned.

By 3:30, everybody is on the worry wagon with me, too tense to go to sleep but also too full of scares about car accidents and muggings for them to want to talk much. We're like twelve parents waiting for a teenage kid: everybody knows what everybody else is thinking, but maybe if they don't mention it, it won't be true.

Then, at quarter to 4:00, it happens: Jerry walks in the window. Everybody's back is to it, but it's a cinch the window never opened: it had been painted shut years ago and it was still painted shut that morning. Not only that, but after he's in the room, he just keeps on walking through as if he's going to bed. He doesn't say a word to anybody. In fact, he looks like he's in some kind of trance.

Now we're really scared, but for a whole new reason: not only do we all know the window didn't open but also we happen to be in an apartment on the fourth floor where the only fire escape is off the kitchen in the back. One of the girls lets out a scream.

This snaps Jerry out of whatever he was in. "Hey, don't worry," he says. "It's only me. Time to hit the sack." Not a word about where he'd been, let alone any explanation of how he walked in out of thin air. Just, "See you in the morning," and into the bedroom. I don't think he even knew what he'd done.

From then on though, there was definitely something different about him: when he talked again in the park the next day, he hit the dying business harder than he ever had in public. Needless to say, he had pretty much the same crowd as the day before, but between the death emphasis and the way he talked in riddles, he lost them completely by mid-afternoon.

It was almost as if he was trying to get rid of them. At the beginning, they were obviously feeding him straight lines. You know. Like, yesterday he'd shown he could solve the hunger problem single-handed; why didn't he run for office or something and do it in a big way? All he kept saying though, was how that wouldn't solve anything. Even if people got food miraculously, he told them, they would still die eventually. The food they really needed to be filled with was something that would make a real break with the old order—something that would actually bring in the new order if they ate it. In fact, he said, unless they were filled with him, they would just stay dead forever. If they fed on him, though, he would raise them from death for good.

Even those of us who were close to him had never heard that one before, so we had no more clue than the crowd what he was talking about. So much so that after they all got fed up and wandered off, he took one look at our faces and said, "Are you guys going to split, too?"

Mostly to cheer him up, I said, "Of course not, Jerry. Where else would we go? If there is a new order, it's a cinch you're the only one who can bring it in." I have to admit, though, that I didn't feel as cheerful as I sounded. I kept remembering him in that trance after coming in the window—and wondering whether maybe something hadn't permanently snapped.

It hadn't, of course; but since I couldn't shake the idea, it eventually just popped out of me. It was the last week in July, in fact. We're all just sitting around with him one night, when suddenly he decides he wants to do a little debriefing. "The twelve of you hear people's reactions more than I do," he says; "who do they say I am?"

We start telling him that some of them call him a guru or a magician, and some of them even think he's his cousin Spencer come back to life. (I don't want to get into it now, but as it turned out, Spencer not only ended up in a mental hospital right after his ceremony with Jerry; he died there after being knifed by another patient.) Anyway, Jerry just listens to the different reactions for a while and then says, "Well, so much for outside information. Who do *you* say I am?"

Again, maybe because I know he took Spencer's death harder than most of the rest knew, I try to be cheerful. "You're God," I say. "And you've got the new order right in your pocket."

His first reaction to this, as far as I'm concerned, is kind of extreme. I mean, he knows me as well as anybody: I just babble along, mostly repeating what I've heard. He, however, acts as if I've just said something new and brilliant. Almost with tears in his eyes, he says, "You're the best thing that ever happened to me, Marvin. There's no way on earth I ever really hoped you'd believe that. I couldn't have picked a better chief witness." But then, without even batting an eye, he suddenly turns grim. "It's going to happen soon, you know—my death, I mean. And unfortunately, one of you is going to make it happen."

Since this strikes me not only as off the wall but also as completely ridiculous, I decide to just keep trying to be cheerful. "C'mon," I say, "don't talk like that. We all love you. You'll probably be around for years."

"You know something, Marvin?" he says, looking at me hard, "you're a real pisser. I never met anybody in my whole life who could be as right and as wrong as you are in two breaths. Believe me, I'm going to die soon, and I'm going to die because of one of you. If you want stay with me, don't kid yourself that's not the way it's going to be."

Later on, after Jerry had actually died and risen, I sort of apologized to him one day for all the times—including the one I was sorriest about, which I'll come to later—when I talked without thinking. "I guess when they handed out mouths," I said, "they forgot the 'off' switch on mine."

"I don't think so Marvin," he laughed. "It's probably there. But one thing's for sure: nobody's going to find it in a hurry."

9

It was on August 6th that the second and biggest turning point in Jerry's thinking came.

For about eight days after he got mad at me, he was edgier than I ever saw him. For one thing, he kept harping on how soon he was going to die. But for another, he started doing something I never heard him do before: swear. He not only looked angry, he talked that way too. Before then, even when he was tearing apart the old order, he was always good-natured, if not downright funny about it. Now though, he sounded feisty, even mean. "They're embarrassed by me, aren't they?" he said about one crowd in particular. "Dumb bastards! As long as you give them a lot of pap and a couple of cures, they love you. But tell them what's really coming down the pike and they treat you like some kind of sleazy half-wit. Shit! I should be embarrassed by *them*!"

Anyway, he went on pretty much in that same vein right up to August 6th. After supper that night though, he took a nap and when he got up he seemed to be his old self again. "Marvin," he says to me, "why don't we go for a walk? Get the green meanies out of our brains." So he takes me and the two Waters kids and out we go.

It's a hot, still night. Even though it's after midnight, there are lots of people on the street trying to manufacture breezes by walking; but being in a crowd doesn't seem to be what Jerry has in mind. "C'mon," he says. "Let's try the park. I know someplace nobody goes."

When we get there we follow the footpaths for a while and

then, at a dark place, he suddenly turns off across some open ground and starts walking up a rise. At the top, it's still black as pitch, but at least there's a little breeze so the three of us just flop on the grass and enjoy it. Jerry, though, stays standing as if he's looking around for somebody.

What happened next is so weird that neither I nor the Waters kids ever even talked about it with each other, let alone anyone else, until after he actually rose from the dead: we're lying there in the dark, not seeing anything or anybody, and very gradually I realize I'm beginning to be able to make out Jerry—even though he's at least fifteen or twenty feet away. At first I just figure it's my eyes adjusting, but that isn't it, because I still can't see my own hand. Then, little by little, he gets brighter and brighter. I know it sounds like a funny comparison, but what it was like was watching an electric broiler heat up: it goes from dark to light so slowly that for a while you're not quite sure anything's happening, but then eventually there's no doubt about it. The difference here though, is that a broiler stops at a certain brightness and Jerry didn't. He kept lighting up, clothes and all, until it was almost blinding to look at him.

How long this took, I have no idea; but by and by I'm aware that two other guys, almost as bright as he is, have showed up— and that they're talking to him. Not loud enough for me to hear everything they're saying: all I get is an occasional reference to his "exit," whatever that is—always followed by the words "not much longer now." That's all I can remember because in addition to their speaking softly, I get very sleepy for some reason and actually drop off. So do the Waters kids.

Whether we sleep for minutes or hours, I have no idea; in any case, when we wake up, the two guys are still there talking so I just watch—again, for I don't know how long. Eventually, though, I find myself getting more and more fidgety and scared. Not exactly of something bad happening, I don't think—it was more like being afraid that what was happening in front of me was taking me so far away I would never get back to my ordinary life again. Being Marvin though, I'm not so scared that I don't try to cut it down to size with small talk. "Hey, Jer," I say to him, "this is incredible. You guys look like a stained-glass window with the sun right behind it. I wish I had a camera."

He doesn't say anything and neither do the two guys. Instead, I hardly get the words out of my mouth before this thick blanket of fog just drops out of nowhere right on top of us. Naturally, with the light pouring out of the three of them into the fog, it's like trying to see with your high beams on: it's worse than being in the dark. So there we sit, having lost sight of everything, when out of the middle of the fog comes this loud voice. "Hey! Why don't you just shut up and listen to Jerry?" it says. "He's all I have in mind." And with that, the fog disappears and we're back in the dark—no shining guys, not even any Jerry that I can see. 'You still there, Jer?" I call to him.

"Sure," he says, as if nothing had happened.

"Alone?" I ask him.

"Yeah," he says. "Alone."

This makes me a little less scared, so I get curious about the voice: "Who said about 'listening to Jerry'? One of the other two?"

"No, Marvin. Let's not talk about it, huh?"

This sounds final, so I drop my next question about who the guys were and let it go at that. We walk back down to the path and head for the apartment without saying a word. Finally, when we're halfway up the stairs, Jerry breaks the silence "Not a word, okay?" he whispers. "Scout's honor?"

"Scout's honor," I tell him. And that, believe it or not, was that.

From then on though, everything seemed different. He still could get feisty, but mostly he was just preoccupied and sad. That, and what I can only describe as being finally out of patience—as if he didn't really much care what he did any more. As far as I could tell, he still didn't know how his death was actually going to happen, but he seemed to have stopped taking the precautions against it that an ordinary person would. For one thing, he hardly ate. For another, he crossed streets practically with his eyes closed, as if he was just hoping some cab driver would run him down and get it over with. For a third, though—and again, I don't think he really knew the effect it was going to have—he went to a funeral and finally got Curtis down on his case for good.

That was what got it all rolling, but before I tell you about it, I should fill you in about the way Jerry's preoccupation affected the rest of the witnesses. It certainly didn't bring out the best in them. With him sort of all wrapped up in himself, they didn't know what to do with their time; so they got into these long arguments about what it was going to be like when the new order came in, and even which of them would be the most important and who would be allowed to stand right next to Jerry when it happened. I stayed out of it as much as I could, partly because I thought it was stupid and partly because I was already the chief witness, for whatever that was worth. Mainly, though, I think it was because of my reaction to the weird business in the park.

Curtis, by the way, stayed out of it too, and the others were pretty quick to say that was because he already thought he was the only important one anyway. But I've always wondered whether, if he'd been there in the park with us that night, maybe he wouldn't have done what he did. I mean, the effect it had on me was finally to convince me that just listening to Jerry—not understanding him, not figuring out what he was up to, not even particularly helping him get it done—was all that mattered. The impression I came away with after the fog disappeared and we were there alone with Jerry was that the new order was entirely his baby and that all I had to do was wait for him to deliver it. I wish I could say that the way I behaved through it all was as good as my impression, but it wasn't. Maybe, though, that was just too much to hope for. Maybe nobody could ever really change enough to deserve the new order. Maybe, even if Curtis had been there, he still would have to have done what he did. Maybe . . .

But that's neither here nor there. What I started to say about Curtis was that if he could have convinced himself to just listen, it might have at least dawned on him that maybe Jerry wanted his trust more than he needed his help.

"Okay, Curtis," I tried to tell him one night. "So the dying thing is an absolutely beautiful idea. But it's *Jerry* who's supposed to be the answer, not some brilliant notion, right? So if he comes around tomorrow and tells me he's going to bring in the new order by becoming Chairman of the Joint Chiefs of Staff instead of by dying, I for one am not about to think there's any point in arguing with him. If he's it, he's it. If he isn't, there's nobody else to go to anyway."

"But dammit!" Curtis yells, pounding his chair arm. "It was *his idea*."

"We've been through this before, Curtis," I tell him. "It never gets us anywhere. I just wish I could tell you about something that happened to Jerry when just me and the Waters kids were with him. Maybe then you'd understand."

This, obviously, was a mistake—one of those brilliant M. H. Goodman oil-on-troubled-water jobs that ends up being gasoline on a bonfire.

"Wonderful," Curtis snarls. "Wonderful. And why can't you tell me? Jerry warn you not to?"

I can't bring myself to admit that he did, so all I do is give Curtis as small a nod of my head as I can manage. "I'm sorry," I say. I really was, too, but he shakes the apology off.

"No you're not," he says, putting on a sick smile. "Or if you are, why do I still get the feeling I'm being set up? Ever think about that, Marvin? Ever think about that?"

"No," I said. "Not at all."

Afterwards, though, I thought about it a lot.

10

I'll tell you one other thing I thought about. Even though Jerry never gave the idea any real encouragement, people were always assuming that the new order would make all kinds of demands on them—as if it couldn't come in unless they cooperated with it perfectly or developed a red hot trust in it. More and more, I decided that was all a lot of bunk.

As far as I could see, people's virtues or the lack of them had nothing to do with anything. Take my wife, Shirley, for example. She gave the new order zero cooperation and even less trust, and yet in at least one instance she was more tuned into it than I was. I know it's a small point, but after that scene with Jerry and the two guys in the park, I couldn't help remembering her wisecrack: "What does he do, glow in the dark?" So what if she only meant it as a zinger at me? She said it before it happened, didn't she? Which, no matter what her reasons were, puts her skepticism a couple of notches above my trust, at least as far as the facts are concerned.

Or take Curtis, who was sort of Shirley in reverse. Shirley, who's a well of cynicism, perceives something in spite of herself; Curtis, who as far as I'm concerned is a mountain of perception, ends up losing it all because of his arrogance and jealousy. I mean, there just isn't any *proportion*: worse or better, more perceptive or less—none of it seems to matter all that much. And it certainly makes mincemeat out of any attempt to keep score.

It's just one more proof that what Jerry was up to wasn't dependent on anybody but himself. The new order worked regardless of other people's faults—as matter of fact, in Curtis's case it even

worked because of them. Maybe this is a funny illustration, but I
finally decided that what it was most like was being on the dance
floor of a cruise ship during a storm. You know: there are some
terrific dancers, and there are some average ones, and there are a
good half of them who have two left feet. But when the ship rolls,
the tilt overrides everybody. All of them, good, bad and indifferent,
go lurching to the low side of the dance floor in a whole new kind
of maneuver that has nothing to do with anybody's dancing—and
which, if they can just relax about it, is a hell of a lot of fun. Unfortunately, Curtis was no good at relaxing. I only hope some day
he'll see that even with him standing there refusing to go along, he
was still in the dance anyway. It may have worked out badly—and
he sure as hell had no fun—but it did work out.

Again, though, I'm getting ahead of the story, so let me pick
up where I left off. Even though I haven't said anything about it so
far, right from the beginning Jerry got a certain amount of media
coverage. It was inevitable, I guess. You can't do cures and feed
five thousand people with an anchovy pizza without somebody trying to hype you. Not that the big papers or magazines gave him
much play. Most of his miracles, even the raising of the girl in the
hospital, were so laid back that it was easy to write them off as hys-
teria, or psychological cures, or coincidences, or even as fakes. The
sensation rags and scandal sheets, however, sandwiched him right
in there between the frozen babies and Princess Di losing thirty-
five pounds. So for what it was worth, by the time summer rolled
around he was not exactly an unknown.

Not that he took the publicity seriously. Lots of times he'd try
to laugh it off by poking fun at the young-man-with-miraculous-
powers stuff. "I'm lucky I'm only being covered as if I were a two-
headed pig," he said once. "If I ever got serious journalists on my
case, they'd analyze the hell out of what I'm doing. This way, at
least it's good for a laugh." Still, it galled him. Especially the solemn
stuff about a "miraculous solution to the world hunger problem"
that they ran after the feeding. Eventually, even local TV picked
up on that one: they began hounding him to appear on talk shows.
He kidded about that too, of course. "Think of it," he said: "the

new order, slotted right in there between a sex-change specialist and the author of *A Hundred and One Desserts with Granola*, all in thirty minutes, even counting commercials."

This kind of thing went on straight through July and August—so much so, that by September he was mostly lying low. Since that didn't seem to make much difference to the vultures though, he finally decided that getting out of town for a while was the only thing to do. "Ever since the river caught fire, Cleveland thinks it has to produce a sensation a week," he kidded. "Let's go someplace dull."

"Good idea," I tell him. "Where do you want to go?"

"Cincinnati," he says.

"You sure you want it *that* dull?" I kid him back. "Cincinnati is a place to be *from*, not to go *to*. Besides, in September, the air is so thick, they have to cut it in blocks and haul it across the river to Kentucky just so they can walk through the streets. George Washington wouldn't even sleep there. Claimed the place wasn't fit for human habitation, only for pigs."

Jerry laughs. "Never trust George Washington's recommendations. Actually, he didn't sleep anywhere: he had these wooden teeth with a bad fit and the pain kept him awake all night. I still say Cincinnati."

So, on September 17th (finally, I can give you a time sequence I'm sure of), he gets a few of us together—Greg Waters, Dieter Schmidt, Carol Peterson and myself—and we drive down. In my Avis rental, naturally. We put up in a nothing motel, bring in Big Macs and Chicken McNuggets, and relax for the first time in months. Even Jerry. It was like going all the way back to the beginning, before everything got so mysterious and heavy.

It lasted for only two days. Late each night, I made a point of calling back to Cleveland just to see how everybody was. On the first night I had a typically one-sided conversation with Timmy Waters; but on the second, the 19th, Jennifer answers the phone. I'm glad to hear her of course, but she sounds as if she's going to burst into tears any minute. As it turns out, her sister Marjorie's son is in the hospital with a recurrence of his heart problem. (I should fill you in: Margie is fifteen years older than Jennifer; her son Johnny is nineteen and has had a heart defect ever since he was born. Even as a little kid he had about five operations to correct a missing valve or something. The doctors said at the time he probably wouldn't live to an old age, and he wasn't exactly a well kid all along. Still, you're never prepared.)

All Jennifer actually says about this though, is that I should please tell Jerry. Obviously, she expects he'll come right back to Cleveland. As a matter of fact, I myself expect he will too: Jerry knew Margie pretty well by now and he especially liked the kid, who also was crazy about him. When I hang up and give the news to Jerry though, I get a very funny response.

"I guess we pack it in here and go back tomorrow, huh?" I ask him.

"No need to, Marvin," he says with a wave of his hand. "It's probably one of those desperate but not serious things."

"But Jennifer said you should . . ."

"I bet she didn't, Marvin. I bet she only said to tell me, right?"

"Well . . ." I mumble. "I just thought . . ."

"That's okay," he says. "Let's just wait a while, all right?"

I figure he knows something I don't know, so I just drop the subject, expecting to hear that Johnny's all better the next time I call. I mean, if Jerry could cure my mother-in-law with a miracle from Cleveland to New York, why not Margie's son with one from Cincinnati to Cleveland?

So we stay put, and when I make my call on the night of the 20th, the news, while it's still not good, is not particularly bad either: he's about the same but resting pretty well. But then on the 21st, right in the middle of lunch, Jerry suddenly looks up from his Filet-O-Fish and says, "I think we should go back to Cleveland."

"You mean, now?" I ask him. "Why?" I'm assuming, of course, that Johnny's going to be okay, so the only thing in my mind is the original reason for coming to Cincinnati in the first place: to let the media forget him for a while. "I think your TV fans need a little more time to cool off," I tell him. "A couple more days here won't hurt."

Whatever answer I expected to that, he never gave it to me. Instead, he starts talking in riddles: "You've got twelve hours of daylight today, Marvin, and you can see where you're going. But anybody who has to stumble around in the dark is not in such good shape."

"What's that mean?" I ask him.

"Johnny's asleep," he says. "But I'm going to go wake him up."

Since this leaves me just as much in the dark as before, I decide the best I can do is go along with it. "Oh," I say. "You think that's such a good idea? I mean, doesn't he need all the rest he can get?"

"Nah, Marvin," he says. "Johnny's dead. And frankly, I'm glad I wasn't there—for your sakes, so you can finally trust. But let's go to him now, okay?"

Needless to say, I get right on the phone to Margie. She isn't home, but whoever is tells me she's at the undertaker's. Johnny, it turns out, died suddenly at 10:00 that morning. When I hang up, though, instead of blurting the news right out, I get this funny mental picture: it's of a circle with the top half light and the bottom half dark. I'm sitting in the top half eating a Filet-O-Fish and Johnny is in the bottom half stumbling around. For some reason I have the feeling this means we're supposed to get to him right away, so I say as much to Jerry when I give him the news. All he says though, is, "There's no rush, Marvin. Tomorrow morning will be fine."

Which it was, but only if you call it fine to start leaving at 6:00 and not get going tell 10:00. In any case, when we finally do get to Margie's house in Cleveland, it's going on 2:00, the place is surrounded by cars, and she's just backing hers out of the driveway. Jerry jumps out to stop her, practically getting himself hit in the process; but when she sees who it is, she gets out and just lets him put his arms around her for a good long hug. I park, and when I get over to them, I hear her saying to him, "If you'd been here, you know, he wouldn't have died. Still, I'm glad you came. I know you'll do what you can."

She says this in a completely flat way: not resentful, but not particularly hopeful, either. He just keeps holding her, pats her on the shoulder and says, "Don't worry, Margie, he'll rise."

At that point, she pulls away from him and puts on the kind of smile you give a kid who means well but probably won't deliver. She's been around Jerry long enough to have heard the dying and rising business a dozen times, so mostly as if *she* was trying to cheer *him* up, she says, "I know, Jerry. When the new order comes in, we all will. Still . . ."

Jerry, however, just cuts her off. "*I'm* the new order right now, Margie. Johnny believed that, so it's all okay. Where's Jennifer?"

"In the house," she says, "getting ready to go to the funeral home. I'll go tell her you're here."

"Do it quietly, huh?" Jerry says. "I don't need a mob around."

He could have saved his breath. When the houseful of people who were inside with Jennifer see the way she jumps up and runs, they follow her right out the door, falling all over her to make sure she's all right.

That's another one of the unequal things the new order is going to have to do some fancy rolling and pitching to turn into a fun dance. Here's Margie who was pretty plain to begin with and who is now thick in the middle besides. She's lost her son, but since everybody knows she's a real trouper, they let her jockey her own car out of the driveway and don't think twice about where she's going. But there's the kid's Aunt Jennifer, who's a knockout, and a world-class weeper in the bargain: she makes one little move and an army of sympathizers gets mobilized. Jerry used to say that in the new order the lion would lie down with the lamb. It seems to me that an equally neat trick is going to be the mother and the aunt.

Anyway, Jennifer comes tearing down the steps like something off a historical novel jacket and throws herself in Jerry's arms. "If only you'd been here," she sobs—and repeats it about six times before getting around to ". . . Johnny wouldn't have died." Jerry is busy paying attention to her all this while, so he doesn't notice the

crowd around him until she calms down a little. But when he does
. . .

Half of them are crying worse than Jennifer; but for some reason, instead of giving them any sympathy, this god-awful black look
comes over his face. In fact, he gets almost nasty. "C'mon, c'mon,"
he snaps. "Where's this funeral parlor? There's no point standing
around here."

Somebody tells him it's Carlino's, which is only a couple of
blocks away; but in spite of what he just said, he just stands there
looking like somebody turned him to stone. Then—of all things—
he starts crying himself. This I don't understand at all, but the
crowd is not short of opinions. "Poor guy," some woman says. "He
must really have been fond of Johnny." "It's crazy though," somebody else pipes up. "If he was, why didn't he come sooner? If he
could cure strangers, why couldn't he do as much for a friend?"

Eventually though, everybody gets their act together and
makes a kind of straggly procession to the funeral home with
Margie and Jerry in front and the rest of us strung out behind
them for about a block. When we get there, we all stand around
outside—waiting, I suppose, for Jerry to go in first. But he doesn't.
He gets the black look again and lets out what sounds like a dis-
gusted sigh. I think to myself, if he doesn't get a grip on himself
soon, he's going to come completely unstuck. Maybe Curtis was
right about telling him to stay away from funerals. Or maybe it was
Curtis telling him that's ungluing him. Who knows?

We stand there a little longer while Jerry sighs a couple of times
more, and then Margie says to him in this sympathetic voice, "If
nothing's possible, Jerry, I'll understand. I mean, what with his
being embalmed and all . . ."

"That isn't it, Margie," he says, cutting her off. "Just trust me.
C'mon in. You'll see."

We follow them inside to the room they've got Johnny in, and
Jerry walks straight over to the casket. For about a minute, he just
stands there staring at the ceiling while everybody gets quieter and
quieter; but then, in a loud voice he speaks straight to the body
in the casket. "Hey, Johnny! Time to get up." And sure enough,

the dead kid sits bolt upright, just as if an electric shock went right through him.

What can I tell you? I've said it before, but as far as I'm concerned, miracles are always half funny, if not half-assed. I mean, look at it: only the top part of Johnny's casket lid is open, so when the kid finally realizes what the bottom half of his body is stuck in, he starts to panic. My own reaction, typically, is to think of something stupid: I've heard of people being too cheap to bury both the jacket *and* the pants to a suit, so I wonder if the kid isn't going to be embarrassed as well as scared. Jerry, though, just turns to one of the undertaker's flunkies and barks at him, "C'mon, what are you waiting for, another miracle? Get the other part of the lid open and let him out."

And that, finally, was really and truly that. There was no way of keeping the media out of this one: any cover that Jerry might have had was blown for good. All the other raisings he did might have been debatable—you know: any skeptic who wanted to could say the people involved weren't really dead. But since everybody knows that embalming does the job on you even if nothing else does it first, this one was an open and shut case—or casket, maybe I should say. Once the word got out, everything went out of control. By the time we got Johnny back to the house, reporters were all over the place and the TV stations had the phone ringing off the hook.

Once again, Curtis was right. Just how right—and also, just how wrong—not even he knew that night. But from then on, there wasn't anybody, not even Jerry, who could turn back the tide.

11

The raising of Johnny took place on September 22nd, and from the minute Jerry did it, it was if he resigned himself completely to whatever was going to happen: he just seemed to give up taking the initiative for anything. Everybody noticed that about him; and both Curtis and I, without ever actually talking about it to each other, did what we could to protect him from being carried off in six directions at once.

As I said, the reporters were after him like flies; but between the two of us, we managed to keep them away from him. Not that it made all that much difference. They wrote their stories anyway. If there were facts they couldn't get, they just made them up out of thin air. The story as it came out was part tearjerker and part sensationalism. You know: the sickly child who grows up to be the teenager everybody loves; the self-sacrificing mother who bears up nobly under the shock of his death; and the distraught aunt, who gets more coverage than either of them.

As you might have guessed, the pictures that ran with this garbage were typical—and so was the "story behind the story" that they implied. The one of Johnny was a high school photo, three years out of date, and the one of Margie looked like an old passport shot. But the three of Jennifer were all fresh for the occasion and made her look like an only slightly used million dollars. The captions, of course, billed her as the great and good friend of the young miracle worker, the one for whom he had come tearing back from Cincinnati, the beautiful grief-stricken follower, at whose merest word . . . Well, you can imagine the rest: two dashes of fact and a pitcherful of innuendo. The American public's favorite drink.

It was when they got around to Jerry himself, though, that they got really creative. There was nothing at all about the new order; just a lot of Clark Kent/Superman stuff on the cooking school graduate who had powers beyond those of mortal men and blablablah—and who, if he would only put them to use, could be the answer to the world's prayers. The public eats that kind of thing up, too, I guess, but it seems to me you don't have to be very brilliant to figure out that having a guy on the loose who can reverse everybody's death is not something an already overpopulated world would pray for if it was in its right mind. Besides, Jerry never once said he was going to make a program out of raising corpses. He talked about giving people a new life, not about dragging them back to the old one. Sure, he raised a few of them; but only, I think, as a kind of sign of the new order, not as the new order itself.

But that's neither here nor there. By the time the stories hit the papers the next morning, Jerry might as well have been somebody who had just invented an electronic zapper he planned to market for eliminating grief on earth. And, since the whole business was now absolutely impossible for TV to pass up, the studios started phoning twice as often. Once again, Curtis and I ran the best interference we could. I just fobbed them off with any excuse I could think of on the spot, but he got practically nasty with them. "Since it's not at all about what you will inevitably and stupidly try to make of it," he told them, "we are simply not going to subject ourselves to misrepresentation. Don't call us," he said sarcastically, "and don't waste even a minute thinking we'll call you." Eventually, though, a call came when the both of us were out of the room, and Jerry picked it up.

I came in just in time to hear him say, "Oh, well. Why not? What time do you want me there?" He hung up, and I just looked at him, shaking my head. But all he said was, "Not to worry, Marvin. What will be, will be. It'll all work out one way or another." Then he put on a weak version of a bright look and said, "Tell you what. Let's all eat out tonight. We could go to that Chinese place of yours. What do you say?" I just said, "Okay, but let me arrange it in their private room, huh? More fishbowls, we don't need."

What Jerry had accepted on TV, of course, was enough to give Curtis apoplexy. Even as far as I was concerned, it couldn't be anything but a disaster: a segment on a 9:00 A.M. talk show—vicarious experience time for housewives in curlers whose husbands were finally out of the house. "You realize what it's going to be like, don't you?" I told Jerry. "Wall-to-wall sentimentality. Hot and cold running heartbreak plus all the false hope they can stir into it. You're going to have every parent of a dead kid in Cleveland breathing down your neck by the time you get home. Not to mention wives of murdered cops and burnt firemen. It's a no-win situation: if you don't raise the dead, their relatives will lynch you; if you do, the undertakers will. You thought about any of that?"

"Nah, Marvin," he says. "I think I just decided to stop thinking altogether. Why fight city hall?"

12

As you might suspect, supper that night wasn't exactly a fun affair. Everybody was there, but Jerry was practically out of it for most of the meal. He made a little toast at the beginning, holding up his beer and saying how glad he was to have the chance to eat this meal with us, but after that he just said a few words every now and then to me or Greg Waters who were on either side of him. Curtis, who was at the other end of the table, said nothing and left as early as he could.

At the end of the meal, though, Jerry raps on a glass with his chopsticks and gets everybody's attention. Then he takes this one pancake that's left over from my Moo Shu Pork, holds it up, and says, "See this?" For a second, I think he's going to make some kind of joke, but then I realize he's dead serious. "This is me," he says—and tears it right in half.

I don't think I have to tell you, but that hit me smack between the eyes. Nothing at all happened in the room, but suddenly I have this absolute certainty he's as good as dead. He just goes on in a perfectly natural way though, passing half of the pancake to me and the other half to Greg. "All of you take a little and eat it," he says. "It's something to remember me by." Then he takes his glass of beer and says "To life, okay? Everybody take a sip. Something else to remember me by." Nobody says a word, of course. We just pass the pancake and the beer around till they're gone—once again, it's something that's got "final" written all over it—and we just wait, hoping for some better explanation I guess. It doesn't come, though. After a long silence, Jerry pushes back his chair, stands up and says, "C'mon. Time to get going."

We go home for what I consider one of the longest nights on record. As far as I know, Jerry never slept at all; he just alternated between pacing the floor and sitting in a chair. The rest of us tried to stay awake and keep him company but we all kept dozing off. A couple of times he said something to me and woke me up, but I fell right back to sleep and can't remember a word he said—just the vague feeling I had that I was letting him down. Eventually though, it got light, somebody made coffee, and pretty soon it was time to get ourselves ready to be at the studio by 8:15.

I drove Jerry and Greg and a couple of the others over in my car. I offered Curtis a ride, but he said he'd rather drive himself and went on ahead. Greg Waters had called Barbara, Jerry's mother, the night before and invited her to come along, so what with having to go halfway across town to pick her up, and then running into the morning rush on the freeway, by the time we got Jerry to the TV station it was twenty to nine. They just whisked him away to the makeup room and shunted the rest of us into the studio. I never even had a chance to tell him to break a leg or something; the ride over in the car, it turned out, was the last time I was ever with him in the old way. It doesn't matter now, of course, but I still feel bad about that: it was the end of so much that it was hard to see even what happened later as a beginning.

Still, that's getting ahead too, so let me just go on with what happened in the studio. I don't know if you've ever hung around such places, but personally I find them fascinating in a strange way. It's as if there are two different worlds going on right in the same room, one phony and the other real. The real world is the one behind the cameras: there's the director and the producer's assistants and the cameramen, and they're all drinking coffee, talking ball scores and making "in" jokes with each other about the clowns in the control room or who made out with whom at a party last night. The phony world is the empty set on the other side of the cameras: for one thing, it's all front and no back—and even in front, there's only water, not coffee, in the cups. But for another thing, when the host finally does come in, it gets less real instead of more: he's got all these typed pages about books he hasn't read and people he doesn't know from Adam, and all he cares about is getting the stuff on the pages turned into the right number of minutes' worth of sound. Even if he had Adam himself sitting there, all he'd care about was getting him off before the pantyhose commercial. If they never got to the part about the apple, so much the worse for Adam.

The guy who interviews Jerry is like that in spades, a pushy character with all the depth of a coffee stain, whose only fear is dead air: it's a talk show, so even if he does all the talking, it's better than silence. Oh sure, he has some idea about where the interview should go; it should tug the hell out of the heartstrings of the women at home behind the ironing boards. But beyond that, he's bound and determined only to keep his gums bumping.

His plan for Jerry has three ingredients: an intro about Johnny's sickness and Margie's heroism (neither of them, thank God, let themselves be suckered into appearing); then a buildup about Jerry's delay in getting there, and the embalming, and what that does to people; and then, finally, the straight line.

"It would seem, Jerry," he says to him, "that you stayed away deliberately, just so there'd be no question that Johnny had irreversibly . . . er, passed on. Was that it?"

He's hoping, I guess, for a long spiel, but all Jerry does is shrug a little and say, "More or less." Since he doesn't volunteer any more, Mr. Shallow plunges right ahead.

"In other words, Jerry, you wanted to prove not only to others, but to yourself, that your powers would work even after an absolutely unquestionable death experience."

"No," Jerry says. "I didn't have to prove anything—and certainly not to myself."

"You mean, you knew all along that they would work?"

"Look," Jerry says with a little edge, "all this 'powers' talk is misleading. It's not some bunch of forces that did it; it was *me*. Johnny rose because *I'm life*, not because I've got a clip of batteries in my pocket."

Needless to say, this goes completely over the guy's head, so he just rephrases the question. "Well, let me put it this way: you knew all along that *you* could do it. Is that right?"

"Yes," Jerry says, and goes silent again.

"But *how* did you know? And—for what is obviously the sixty-four-thousand-dollar question—*how* did you do it? Is it just a physical phenomenon, or does it involve extraterrestrial principles—or is it even, perhaps, something completely spiritual?"

Mr. Coffeestain, obviously, doesn't know enough about any of those categories to fit in an answer even if he got one, so Jerry pulls him up short with a question. "Why does *how* matter?"

"Er . . . I'm afraid, Jerry, I don't know exactly what you mean."

"I said, why does *how* matter? I know I can raise the dead. And I know I'm the only one who can. It's not something I'm planning to give courses in."

"But if you care about people—and I'm sure you do, Jerry—wouldn't it be wonderful if you could pass this pow . . . sorry, I mean, this ability on? After all, even with your . . . skill . . . you won't always be around . . . or will you?"

"No," Jerry says. "I don't plan to be."

"Well then, why not share it?"

"Look, I told you, it's not a teachable thing; it's unique to me. *How* I do it is irrelevant, because nobody else is up to it anyway. What good would it do you to learn how Michelangelo sculpted the David? Even if you found out, it wouldn't do you any good: you're not Michelangelo."

"But I'd still love to know—and I'll bet every viewer out there would too. Isn't there anything you can tell us about how you actually raised Johnny from the dead?"

"Well, okay," Jerry says suddenly with a bashful smile as if he's relenting. "I take the old dead Johnny and I knock away everything that isn't a risen Johnny, and presto, you've got a risen Johnny. Simple."

By now of course, Mr. Blot realizes he was set up for one of the oldest jokes in the world and Jerry is just sitting there looking sort of pleased. Not for long though, because the rest of the interview is devoted to what amounts to a lecture to Jerry on how this is no laughing matter and how he shouldn't trifle with the sincere griefs and emotions of real people—which, considering that the lecture was being delivered by a real horse's ass, I thought Jerry was very patient with. I mean, it's not every day that God gets a dressing-down on his manners from a talk show host.

Finally though, they flash the guy the signal that a commercial is about due and he goes to the wrapup. "Seriously though, Jerry, tell me one thing. In my mind—and I might add, in the minds of everybody I've talked to—there's no doubt that you've performed a genuine resurrection from the dead in Johnny's case. I'm sure the question that's uppermost in all our viewers minds is this: are you going to be available—more important, I suppose, are you going to be *willing*—to do this again? People, I think, would really like to know."

"Oh, sure," Jerry says. "Maybe not under quite the same circumstances, but definitely yes. Absolutely."

While the host is getting in the rest of his wrapup, I'm aware of something funny going on in the studio. The phony world in front of the cameras and the real world behind them have suddenly gotten together: the crew is actually scurrying around and talking about what's happened on the set. The girl with the clipboard who showed us in even comes over to me. "I think your friend just blew the roof off this place," she says. "The switchboard is jammed with calls."

"Good or bad?" I ask her.

"You tell me," she says. "The ones that don't want to use him want to expose him as a fake. Maybe you better just get him out of here in a hurry."

At this point, the whole group of us are more or less scattered around the studio. Curtis and I and Greg are sitting on folding chairs right behind the middle camera, Barbara is back in a corner by herself, and the rest are standing up, leaning on whatever they can find. When the girl mentions getting Jerry out in a hurry though, Curtis jumps up, practically knocking over his chair, and says, "I'll take him, Marvin. Out the back way. You and the rest go out the front and make it look as if he's with you. By the time they figure out he's not, I'll have him out of harm's way."

He's moving toward the set before he even finishes this, but suddenly Greg Waters grabs my arm and says, "I don't like it, Marvin. I'm going to stop him and take Jerry with us." I have a feeling I don't particularly like the idea either, but since I can't put a finger on it, as usual I put my mouth to work instead. "No, Greg, let him go," I say. "What can possibly happen in Cleveland at ten in the morning?—besides the river catching fire, I mean. You just go get Barbara and we'll all head for my car."

I quickly get the others together and make a big flurry of leading them out, making sure I turn around every now and then and say Jerry's name good and loud to the group behind me. The last I saw him, he was going out the far door.

He waved.

13

Jerry and Curtis were both killed in a car accident at 10:15.

The rest of us had left the studio just before 10:00, the plan being to take a roundabout way to Barbara's house just to lose anybody who might have followed us and then wait there till Jerry called and told us where he was. On top of that though, I also got myself royally lost, so it was almost eleven by the time we got there. All the way in the car, Barbara just sat in the front seat between me and Greg with her eyes closed, not saying a word.

When I finally pulled up in front of the house, the first thing I see is Maybelle Caldwell standing in the doorway as if she's waiting for us. She starts to totter down the steps the minute she spots the car, so I quick put it in park and jump out to head her off before she falls.

I get to her at the bottom of the stairs and she collapses into my arms. "Jerry's dead," she says in a loud voice. "And Curtis, too. Their car ran into an overpass on the freeway. The police said they must have been doing at least eighty miles an hour. They were killed instantly." And at that she breaks down completely and faints.

By now, Greg is next to me and as he takes her off my hands, my mind flashes back to my not letting him stop Curtis when we were at the studio. All of a sudden, I find myself saying, "Oh, shit, shit, shit," and crying at the same time. By now, everybody but Barbara is out of the car helping Greg get Maybelle into the house, so I go over to see how she is. Since she doesn't make a move to get out, I climb in the passenger's side and sit next to her. "You heard, I guess," I say to her.

She nods her head but she still doesn't talk. I can't think of anything to say either, and for once I actually succeed in keeping my mouth from running on anyway. Finally, after what seems like forever, she breaks the silence. "Do you think you could take care of the funeral arrangements for me, Marvin?"

"Well . . . sure," I say.

"I hate to impose on you," she says, "but I'd appreciate it more than you know."

"Oh, it's no imposition," I tell her. "It's just that even with all his talk about dying, this is the first time I ever thought about his actually having to be buried. You really think it's . . . necessary?"

She says, "Yes, Marvin," and goes silent again.

"Okay, then," I say. "Just tell me where and when and the rest, and I'll take care of everything."

"I want him buried in Stefan's plot," she says, "and I want it done before sundown today. Outside of that, I don't care about the rest. You use your judgment."

The sundown business comes as a surprise to me; but even though it means a lot of scrambling on my part, I decide it's probably a good thing to do. "I think you have the right idea there," I tell her, "burying him today, I mean, before the media get a chance to turn his funeral into a circus."

"Oh," she says. "It wasn't that. I just don't want him embalmed, that's all."

For a second, I'm tempted to rattle on with something about how I don't think this is any time to prove a point, but then it dawns on me that maybe it's just his mother talking, so I skip it. "Right," I say. "Just give me the cemetery deed and I'll do the rest. You might stay near the phone in case I need you for something legal, but otherwise, I won't bother you till I've got it all set up."

As it worked out, we couldn't get him buried till 4:00 that afternoon, so in between making arrangements, I had at least a little time to think—or, better said, to be haunted by two things. The first one was the absolute certainty that Curtis had slammed them into the overpass on purpose. He'd made it clear to me too many times that as far as he was concerned Jerry's dying was the key to everything. So, between the raising of Johnny and the stuff on the talk show about Jerry's apparently being willing to do more of the same, I could only conclude that Curtis decided he just had to force his hand. What the hurry was, I could never understand. I mean, Jerry was human: he would have died some day anyhow. But then, I never exactly understood Curtis. Maybe nobody did, not even Jerry.

That was what led me to the really haunting thing, the thought of the two of them there in the car with Curtis pushing it further and further past the speed limit. Did Jerry notice? Did he draw the obvious conclusion? Did he mention it? Did he try to stop him? I asked myself those questions a dozen times and never came up with anything but blanks. The only thing I decided was that I was lucky I didn't have to actually do anything about Curtis: his family had made their own arrangements for his funeral and I figured that was my cue finally to give the subject of Curtis a wide berth.

As I was saying though, we buried Jerry at 4:00. There was no service. The undertaker offered to say what he called "some words," but Barbara said no, so the whole thing was mostly silence. It was just the group of us standing around watching the undertakers carry the casket to the lowering device, then put it on, then flip the lever that unlocks the gears, and then flip it back when the casket got level with the ground.

This, of course, is when they expect the mourners to throw flowers and go home, but before the undertaker can get his announcement out, Barbara speaks up and says, "Lower it all the way, please. I want to stay here till they fill in the grave."

I don't know what your experience with morticians is but from what I've seen, underneath all their velvet concern for the bereaved is a will of iron about getting their own way—plus a genius for cooking up phony excuses on the spot. "But Mrs. Horvath," this one says, "the men are not ready to do that now. And besides . . ."

This irks the hell out of me, so I cut him off right there. "No

besideses, huh?" I snap at him. "As far as I can see, if 'the men'
are those guys with shovels over there, they look to me like they'd
just love to get this over with and knock off early. So lower it,
okay?" He gives me a nasty smile that has "some day I'll get you,
you know" written all over it, and he flips the lever with a kick of
his foot instead of genuflecting to it like they taught him in funeral
school.

The gears whirr, which is a sort of nice sound after listening
to Mr. Nasty; and then the laborers come, which is even nicer because at least they're not trying to make believe they're hanging
somebody in midair instead of burying him in the ground. They
just shovel quietly because Barbara's there, and before I know it,
the grave is all filled in and they're patting it into a nice mound
with the backs of the shovels. "You want to go now?" I say to Barbara. She nods, and we walk over to my car with the rest following
behind.

Somehow, between her silence and nodding her head, my mind
goes back to driving her home from the studio this morning. "You
mind if I ask you something?" I say. She says no, so I go ahead with
what I'm thinking. "You knew about it even before it happened,
didn't you? About the accident and all, I mean."

"Yes," she says.

"When did you know, though? In the studio? In the car?"

"No, Marvin. I knew about it almost a year ago. The first time
I met Curtis."

Then, finally, she cried.

14

Depending on how you want to look at it, the rest of this story is either not much or absolutely everything, so let me just run it out straight.

The day after Jerry's funeral, nothing happened at all. The group of us never even stayed together—which is peculiar when I think about it now, but at the time it just seemed like a natural thing to do. Nobody wanted anything more than to be left alone with their own thoughts. And to tell the truth, if the rest of them had thoughts that were anything like mine, there was no point in dumping them on other people.

Naturally, I tried to cheer myself up by thinking about Jerry actually rising from the dead, but the harder I tried, the less cheerful I got. More and more, I found myself wondering if he could really bring it off. I mean, it's one thing to talk about dying and rising; but dead is dead, and once you've watched somebody have six feet of dirt shoveled on top of him, the talk seems cheap. It didn't do any good, either, to try to console myself with the thought that Johnny and the others had risen. They'd had a live Jerry around to help them. Jerry had only a dead one. You can say you want to believe somebody's promises, but I guess once you start trying to figure out how they could possibly make good on them, it's all downhill from there. You start thinking you should have more evidence to go on; then you decide what kind of evidence you should have; then, having set yourself up, you go and look for it; and then, when it isn't there, you decide there was probably nothing to believe in the first place.

Late that afternoon, I went to the cemetery. Jerry's grave was exactly the way it was when Barbara and I walked away from it the day before. Even the shovel marks were still perfectly clear. I cried. Then I walked to the nearest bar, had a couple of stiff drinks, and went home to bed.

When I woke up the next morning—late, naturally, and still half in the bag—the whole apartment was full of noise. Everybody was in the living room shouting, "He did it! He really did it!" So, dressed only in a pair of shorts, I run out of the bedroom expecting, I guess, to see Jerry standing right there.

He's not though. Instead, what's happened is that Jennifer and Carol Peterson and Beth Murphy have just come in with a story about how the three of them decided separately to go and put flowers on his grave before they went to work, and how they found the grave completely dug up and Jerry's casket just sitting empty at the bottom.

Since everybody is talking at once—which, with my head pounding already, is a real problem—I yell at them to shut up. "Look," I say when they finally calm down. "How do you know it wasn't robbers or something?"

"To steal what?" Beth laughs. "He never carried money when he was alive: unless you slipped some in his pocket, he sure didn't have any on him for the last two days."

"But why would he rise and not show himself to us? Are we supposed to be witnesses, or aren't we? You sure you didn't see him?" I say to Jennifer. "I mean, did you really look around? With an open mind? He might be . . . well, different, you know."

She just looks me up and down for a minute, then smiles, reaches into her purse, and pulls out what looks like a grimy index card. "I don't think he's going to be different, Marvin; and I'm sure if you keep an open mind, you won't even have to look around. Here," she says, handing me the card. "He left this for you. Right on top of the pile of dirt."

What can I tell you? On one side, in Jerry's best menu printing, it says, "For the Chief Witness." On the other, in his regular handwriting, it says, "Hang in there, Marvin. If nobody's found the 'off' button yet, maybe it doesn't matter. See you soon. J."

"Hah!" I say, suddenly feeling no pain whatsoever. "Here I am, just standing here in my shorts, . . ."

And that, finally and for good, was that.

Finale

Scene I

The Eastern baggage claim at the Cleveland airport, forty days later. Jerry, dressed in a new white sweatshirt and painter's pants, is waiting for Marvin and his brother Howard who are about to arrive on Flight 531 from New York. He is leaning against a pillar when Eugene Fosforos, his old high school social studies teacher, walks up to him.

FOSFOROS: Morning, Jerry.

JERRY: Mr. Fosforos! Well, well. It's been quite a while, hasn't it? You meeting somebody too?

FOSFOROS: Not just yet. I wanted to look you up first. Haven't had a chance to talk to you since your . . . performance. Speaking of which, I must say it's a mystery to me why you even bothered to go through with it.

JERRY: Let's just say I figured it was time.

FOSFOROS: Seems to me it was a waste of time. How many people believe you actually rose?

JERRY: Enough for openers. It'll get better.

FOSFOROS: I doubt it. Especially after you get done with this . . . comic opera exit you've got planned for today.

JERRY: What's wrong with a little comedy? The story has a happy ending; why should I have to grunt and groan my way through the last act?

FOSFOROS: But *ascending*, Jerry! It's so . . . *medieval.*

JERRY: C'mon now, Mr. Fosforos. You know better than that. I mean, look: if I want people to believe that I've brought about the new order all by myself and that they're already risen in me, I have to get out of here. Hanging around will only make them think the job isn't done. Worse yet, they'll convince themselves it's not going to be finished until I zap them one by one. On the other hand, it's not such a hot idea simply to stop appearing, because then they'll be so confused they won't know what to think. So, given the circumstances, it's probably best if I provide them with a visual demonstration of my leaving.

FOSFOROS: Still, though, why this . . . charade?

JERRY: Listen. To you it may be a charade; to me, it's just showing a little respect for the natural limitations of the universe. Anybody wants to leave someplace, he's got a choice of only three directions: up, down, or sideways. For my purposes, however, down is not so hot symbolically—and sideways could lead them to think maybe I had just gone to Cincinnati again. That leaves me with only up.

FOSFOROS: Jerry, Jerry. You disappoint me! You were such a wonderful boy. Bright, of course; but more important, *considerate*. What went wrong? Now you're all cleverness and no heart. You've got a whole world full of misery and the only thing you offer it is a mystery that doesn't alleviate a single pain. You have the power to *help* people; why don't you stay here and do something tangible for them instead of sailing off into the blue and leaving them with nothing but an assurance that they're all right when they're not?

JERRY: Mr. Fosforos, I don't want to be rude, but we've been through this before and we've never gotten anywhere with it. You don't like my ideas about using power and I don't like yours. Why don't we just agree to disagree? I've let you have the whole ballgame here and I'm not about to tell you you can't play it any way you like. But your rules are not my rules and you're not going to sucker me into playing by them just by throwing the word "help" around.

FOSFOROS: You really don't care, do you?

JERRY: I care. It's just that I don't show it your way.

FOSFOROS: What do you mean, *my* way? I'm asking you to do *good*, not evil.

JERRY: That argument won't work either, Mr. Fosforos. We both know perfectly well that you can switch the signs on any help I give them, no matter how good it is. If I raise them from the dead, you get them to turn into snot-nosed celebrities; if I strong-arm them into trying to love each other, you make them think love and ownership are the same thing. Therefore, I just don't play: as long as you're around, even my best pitch is a loser.

FOSFOROS: You *could* revoke my franchise.

JERRY: Nah, Mr. Fosforos. That one's not even tempting. You're part of the ecology here by now. If I clean up this mess at all, I clean it up with you in it.

FOSFOROS: You do realize, don't you, what that means? However little history the world may yet have left, it will very likely be worse than all previous history put together.

JERRY: I realize that, Mr. Fosforos. After all, history was my idea. Maybe I even made a mistake inventing it; but if I did, I made it so long ago, I couldn't undo it now without reneging on everything. So you stay, I stay, the whole works stays. I'm not about to put the arm on anything this late in the day.

FOSFOROS: Oh, my. It's all so depressingly familiar, isn't it? As you say, it never gets us anywhere.

JERRY: Yeah. Too bad. Maybe we should just talk about how I'm going to do my ascension, huh?

FOSFOROS: Why not? At least you *are* entertaining.

JERRY: Fair enough. The plan is this: when Marvin and Howie and the rest get here . . .

FOSFOROS: Excuse me. I know I shouldn't interrupt, but . . .

JERRY: That's all right. Be my guest.

FOSFOROS: Well . . . it's only fair to tell you, I find it fascinating, if incomprehensible, that you seem bent on entrusting your entire . . . representation to that collection of . . . clowns. I mean, not taking away my franchise is all well and good; but handing me such a bush league team to play against is just asking for trouble.

JERRY: We'll see. In any case, as I was saying: when they get here, we're all going to go over to the civil aviation section and . . .

FOSFOROS: Ah! I have it: you're going to sail up in the air like a balloon and disappear from sight. Wonderful!

JERRY: Wrong! I'm surprised at you, Mr. Fosforos. This is the 1990s. You've got to have an effect that has a little technological credibility.

FOSFOROS: What do you have over there? A rocket?

JERRY: Of course not. Only the federal government has rockets; if I let them in the act, they'd really gum it up. Besides, rockets go to outer space: people would accuse me of encouraging pre-Copernican views of heaven.

FOSFOROS: All right, all right. How *are* you going to do it?

JERRY: Simple: a private plane. I chartered it yesterday. When we all get there, I say a short goodbye to Marvin and everybody, and then I climb in and tell the pilot I'm ready to go. He doesn't think anything funny is going on because the charter company has told him he's flying me to Philly, so we taxi around for however long it takes the tower to clear us, and then up we go.

FOSFOROS: That's *it*? Neither of you is ever seen again? You don't care about the pilot's wife and children, or his mother?

JERRY: Mr. Fosforos, stop with the care, will you? This is the fun part. When we're airborne, naturally he has to make some kind of turn to get out of the takeoff pattern and head for Philly. But the plane isn't going to stop with just the turn he wants. It's going to do a complete one-eighty and head straight back over the main runway.

FOSFOROS ; And straight into the next 747 taking off, no doubt. Killing three hundred unfortunate but apparently disposable people.

JERRY: Mr. Fosforos! If I can make a plane to do a one-eighty, I can certainly manage to keep a 747 at the end of the runway for a couple of minutes. Trust me.

FOSFOROS: Really, now.

JERRY: Sorry about that. But as I was saying. There we are, heading right back over the airport. I haven't quite got the next part completely worked out, because if he's too high, I may have to bring him down a little so at least a few people can see what happens. And I haven't figured out exactly what I'm going to tell him—maybe I could say I left something in the airport, or better yet, that I decided not to go to Philly after all. In any case, the crucial thing is that right after that, smack dab over the middle of the field, I open the door and walk out.

FOSFOROS: You . . . walk . . . out . . .

JERRY: Yeah. The pilot, naturally, assumes I've lost my mind and splattered myself all over the runway, so he radios a mayday or whatever. The tower, having seen the door open and a guy walk out, doesn't know what to think: they didn't see him fall, but since they can't take any chances, they close down the whole airport till they're sure there's nobody out there on the ground. Terrific, huh?

FOSFOROS: I'm glad it amuses you.

JERRY: Amuses me? I love it! It's not solemn, it's not important, it's hardly even serious—and above all it's not some big fat good deed you can do a number on. Finally, I get to slip you something so close to a zero that no matter how you switch the signs on it, you'll look silly for even bothering. But listen. You have to excuse me now. That's Marvin and his brother coming down the ramp, so I'd better get this show on the road. See you around, Mr. Fosforos.

FOSFOROS: Not if I see you first, Jerry.

Scene II

The main lobby of the Cleveland airport, twenty minutes after all flights have been suspended due to an accident. Travelers are milling everywhere, complaining about delays, seeking information. Marvin is standing alone downstage right when Eugene Fosforos approaches him.

FOSFOROS: Marvin Goodman! You don't know me, but I'm an old friend of Jerry's. His high school social studies teacher in fact. Good to see you.

MARVIN: Oh. My pleasure. How did you know me, though?

FOSFOROS: Well . . . let's say that anyone who interests Jerry is automatically an interest of mine. He never mentioned me to you?

MARVIN: Not that I can recall.

FOSFOROS: Strange. But then . . . that's Jerry. By the way, what did you think of the . . . er, demonstration he just put on?

MARVIN: I loved it. But then, I like anything he does. You too, I guess, huh? I mean, he must've been some kid in school.

FOSFOROS: I'm afraid he never stopped being a kid in school, Marvin. But that's neither here nor there. I understand he gave you an important position to fill after he was gone.

MARVIN: Yeah. I'm the chief witness to his rising from the dead. Actually though, I have no idea whether it's important or not, since there are also ten others.

FOSFOROS: They all saw him?

MARVIN: Not only saw him: talked to him, touched him—even ate a breakfast he cooked: eggs, kippers, toasted English, the works.

FOSFOROS: Still, I'm sure that in some way your position must be unique. If you've got a minute, I think I could perhaps help you understand it a bit better . . . having known Jerry as long as I have, I mean. He's not always the easiest person in the world to digest.

MARVIN: I gave up trying to digest him a long time ago.

FOSFOROS: Still, I really would like to talk with you about him . . . for old times' sake, if for nothing else.

MARVIN: Oh, well, if you put it that way. Listen. Speaking of Jerry and old times, there's a bar right here in the airport I've got a kind of sentimental attachment to. Why don't we go there?

FOSFOROS: A bar? I wonder if that's quite the right . . . setting for someone in your position.

MARVIN: Why wouldn't it be? I don't want to live there; I just want a drink.

FOSFOROS: You don't think a coffee shop would be a little more . . . suitable?

MARVIN: Nah. A bar is fine.

FOSFOROS: Well, if you say so, Marvin. I just wanted to be sure Jerry would approve.

MARVIN: Listen, if you have to wonder about that, I have to wonder whether we're talking about the same Jerry. C'mon though. I'll buy and you can talk.

(*As the lights dim, they walk upstage, their voices trailing off into the general airport sounds.*)

MARVIN: So you knew him as a high school kid, huh? Tell me, was he always so laid back—so sort of hands-off, I mean?

FOSFOROS: Well, Marvin . . . there was more to Jerry than met the eye. After you and I talk, I think you'll understand that a lot better. What you call his "hands-off" attitude, for instance, probably wasn't meant to be a permanent feature of the message you're responsible for transmitting. People are going to need a lot of help and guidance from you, Marvin; otherwise . . .

Curtain